ENGINES OF ENGAGEMENT

A CURIOUS BOOK ABOUT GENERATIVE AI

by Julian Stodd,
Sae Schatz, and
Geoff Stead

with Donald Clark, Mark Oehlert, and Marc Zao-Sanders

Cover image created by Julian Stodd and Sae Schatz

First published 2023

by Sea Salt Learning, Bournemouth, Dorset, UK

www.seasaltlearning.com • www.julianstodd.wordpress.com

ISBN: 978-1-7384482-0-3 (hardback)

ISBN: 978-1-7384482-2-7 (paperback)

ISBN: 978-1-7384482-1-0 (e-book)

Illustrations, visual design, and typesetting by Sae Schatz, Julian Stodd, Geoff Stead, and Sea Salt Publishing.

CONTENTS

Parts 1 and 2 provide the foundation, including a gentle overview of the technology that underlies Generative AI. Parts 3–6 explore deeper questions, such as the erosion of artistry, fragmentation of truth, and evolution of our organisations. You can read this book in any order; in particular, those already familiar with Generative AI may wish to start with Part 3.

INTRODUCTION

The faint noise of distant engines has turned into a roar. Change is upon us, but where should we turn?

A wave of new technologies allows us to ask questions to which we receive detailed answers, to create art without pens or paint, to compose songs without playing an instrument, to dictate videos without picking up a camera, and to explore our deepest curiosities without travelling beyond our own imaginations.

These new tools are engines of productivity and knowledge, art and artifice.

They challenge our notions of creativity, of expertise, of academia, and of work itself. Increasingly, they feel human (or human-like) and are so prevalent that, in time, the distinction may become abstract: the wisdom of *homo sapiens* amplified by technology through dialogue and augmentation. Indeed, we may become unable to delaminate the experience of technology from the notion of humanity.

These technologies are assistive and supportive but perhaps also directive and prescriptive. They may teach us in the flow, nudge our behaviours, or influence our image of reality.

But, beyond the hype, what's different? Where should we be looking and listening, and what should we be doing right now to shift our mindsets to this new reality? What should we fight? What should we receive as a gift? And what do we stand to lose?

Collectively, we know these technologies, these Engines of Change, as **Generative Artificial Intelligence**. It's a term that describes both how they operate 'behind the curtain' and a certain aspiration for what they may ultimately prove to be.

In addition to a wealth of new texts, images, audio, video, and other increasingly dazzling artefacts and effects, Generative AI has produced a great deal of noise, supposition, and opinion. This partly relates to the technology's seemingly rapid proliferation into the public consciousness and partly to the very human and conversational ways in which the most popular Generative AI tools operate.

Interacting with these systems feels almost natural, personal, and engaging, like a good conversation, and they can seemingly connect us to a range of knowledge, creativity, and storytelling beyond the capability of any human. Through its ease of use and apparent ease of understanding, Generative AI brings to the fore a heady mix of conjecture and hope.

But, like humans, this technology is imperfect. It can be inaccurate in its knowledge, delusional in its logic, and frankly surrealist in its art. At other times, it can be so convincingly articulate that it may lull us into forgetting that it's a machine without conscious thought.

Hence, it's a technology that has rapidly come into conflict with our various systems of understanding, sense-making, and control, conceptions of fairness, and our marketplaces of social currency. Its release has slammed headlong into a mire of legal challenges, ethical questions (and pseudo-ethical conflations), and commercial issues – not to mention environmental and political disruption. Generative AI has landed rapidly but not smoothly.

It's rare to see something erupt into the public consciousness as quickly as Generative AI has and to grow to this scale of idolisation and inspiration, rhetoric and misunderstanding, dogma and doubt without any apparent marketing or promotion. And this is what led us here, to this curious book: a catalyst to pause, reflect, and share – a product of the conversations and musing from our 'campfire'.

THIS BOOK: A CURIOUS THING

There's already a lot of noise around Generative AI, and we don't intend to add to it – at least not unduly. We reserve the right to be both brave and wrong. With that in mind, this isn't a book of answers, but rather one of curiosity and ideas. We intend to walk through the landscape with our eyes open to wonder and doubts.

In this book, we traverse through some of the questions and opportunities that Generative AI compels. We look at how these systems work at a simple level and unpack why they produce gut feelings of both possibility and uncanny fear.

We hope to shine a bit of light on the broader context, to help open our minds to creatively explore the social and organisational impacts that this technology heralds. How might it affect our decision-making, our legacy structures of organisation and education, of knowledge and control? How will it change the ways we think and learn and, in the end, how we perform – not in terms of outsourced tasks or novelty images – but across the fundamental fabric of our lenses of understanding?

This work is both serious and playful. We didn't want to produce a technical guide or a naive list of clickbait observations, and we're also not particularly interested in exploring certainty. Others will give you answers. We're sharing our questions – questions about where we may be going, what we may see on the journey, and what may change in the future.

… which, for the avoidance of doubt, may well be everything.

★ ★ ★

AUTHORS' NOTE

We weren't supposed to be here. Julian, Sae, and Geoff were busy writing a book on Learning Science when we realised that, in those conversations, we were spending an undue amount of time discussing Generative AI. When Julian suggested we pause our other efforts to write a 'quick' book on AI, his co-authors were rightly hesitant of his right-angled thinking. But we agreed to give it a go.

After a few weeks, Julian had grown daunted and unsure, but Sae and Geoff had become enthused, and so it went. Through confusion and optimism, we stutter-stepped ahead over a series of weekly 'happy hour' cafe sessions and a (now quite unwieldy) shared document. And somehow, here we are.

The story of our writing process illustrates the nature, strength, and fragility of our collaborative work. We each bring different knowledge and perspectives and inhabit different everyday realities. Each of us has variously taken the lead in different sections – sometimes to rein the others in, sometimes to challenge us to move further, and sometimes simply to be curious together.

We hope that you engage in this work as a partner in thought, not a passive recipient of wisdom. We've tried to open a space for more measured, and perhaps a bit peculiar, contemplation – and not always of the most obvious concepts. We hope you enjoy it.

Julian Stodd is a writer, researcher, artist, and explorer. His work explores the context of the Social Age, a place where technology has evolved what it means to be human. His work typically exists at the intersection of systems: Social Leadership, Social and Collaborative Learning, and views of Culture, Innovation, and Change held more as social movements than structural affairs. Julian has written seventeen books and works to a principle of #WorkingOutLoud, sharing iterations every day and frequently finding new ways to be wrong.

Sae Schatz is a creative designer of systems, strategies, and artefacts for sense-making. Her professional work resides at the intersection of human cognition and learning, technology, and data. She's lived several lives: working as an assistant professor in academia, a chief scientist in business, and most recently, leading the Pentagon's Advanced Distributed Learning programme to develop AI-enabled and data-driven lifelong learning. Today, she advises governments and other organisations worldwide on using emerging technologies and learning science.

Geoff Stead is a learning technologist, an inventor of products, and a shaper of the creative teams it takes to make them real. He's happiest working in the blend between humans and technology, adapting emerging tools to find better ways to reach or teach learners across the globe. He divides his time between leading Product for MyTutor and advising other EdTech start-ups that are working to make a meaningful difference in the world.

Thank you for engaging with our work.

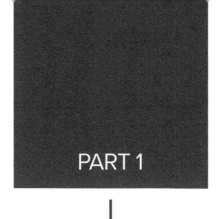

PART 1

The Engines are Here

The recent hype has created an 'Emperor's New Clothes' moment for a lot of us. We may have had some fuzzy notions about AI before, but now, it feels like we're all expected to have informed opinions about how Generative AI, Deepfakes, and Large Language Models will change the world.

So, let's begin at the beginning.

AI is an overarching category for software that does human-like things, such as problem-solving, perceiving the world, making decisions, and learning. We can divide it into sub-fields, including **Natural Language Processing** (which lets computers work with human languages, whether analysing our words or communicating with us in more humanistic ways), **Computer Vision** (which allows computers to 'see' things like humans do, to 'translate' the input from sensors into a perception of the world around them), **Robotics** (which allows for manual interaction with the world, such as machines working in a factory and automated medical devices that assist with precision surgery), and **Machine Learning** (which refers to systems that don't simply have programmed capabilities but can 'learn' from their environments and the information we feed them).

It's useful to understand that not all AI uses Machine Learning. Sometimes an algorithm uses 'Good Old-Fashioned AI' (also called Symbolic AI), which is a rules-based approach. Picture a horde of software developers hunched over small desks, manually typing out decision trees and 'if-then' procedural lists. (If it helps, feel free to imagine helmeted overseers and a faintly Orwellian decor.) For many legacy systems, this handmade approach is sufficient – just not as mind-shattering as what we've achieved through modern, data-driven methods.

Machine Learning is a data-driven approach that involves 'training' algorithms using large data sets. Simply put, Machine Learning algorithms examine many different examples of something – such as millions of pictures of different animals. Over time, the algorithms uncover patterns in those data – for instance, learning to isolate pictures that show a 'cat'. In practice, beyond this simple illustration, once an algorithm finds patterns in a data set, it can use that information to identify hidden trends, find root causes, inform decisions, or make predictions applicable to the given subject matter.

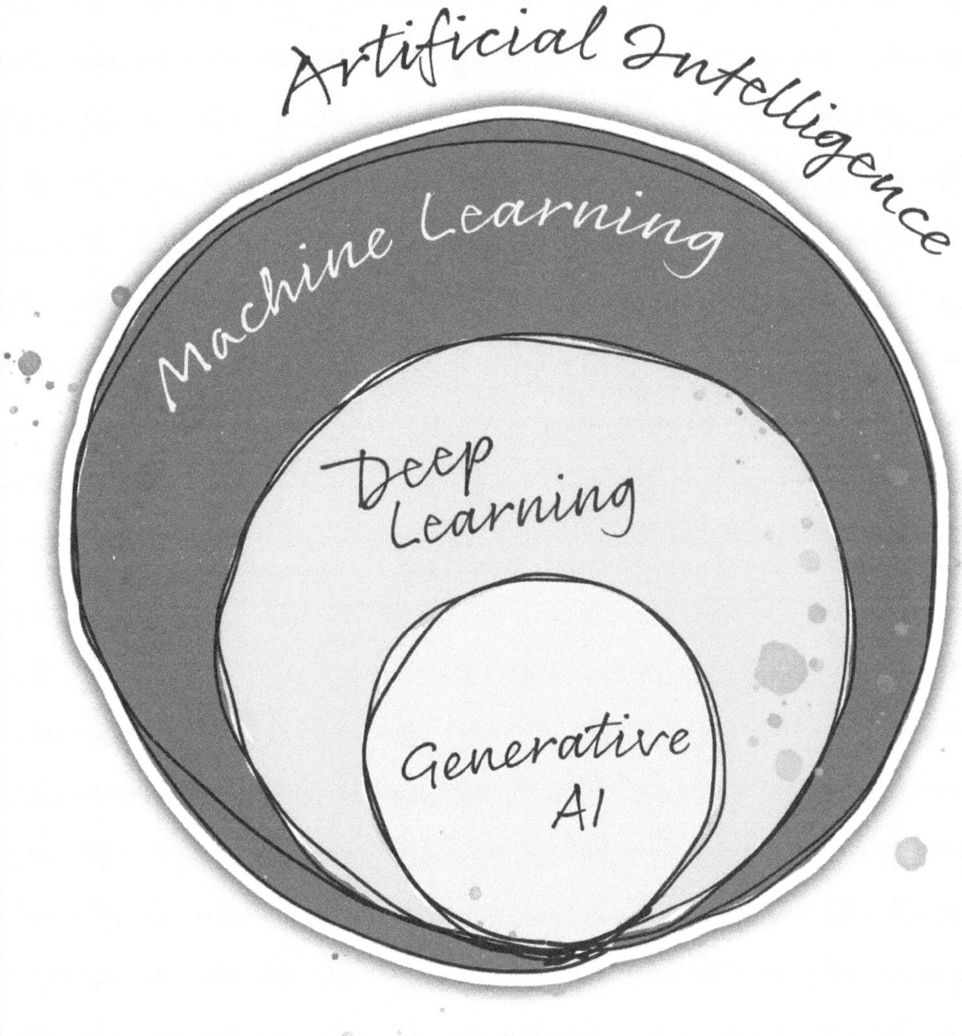

Artificial Intelligence

Machine Learning

Deep Learning

Generative AI

They operate without thunder and fumes
but are nonetheless engines – not of motion
but rather of story and song, of knowledge
and image – quietly changing the familiar,
fracturing certainty, reflecting the world back
to us.

Talking to us.

In dialogue with us.

Drawing us. Singing to us.

Mimicking us.

Watching us.

These systems are so simple as to be
disruptive, so complex as to be misunderstood,
and so powerful as to change the world with a
whisper.

The engines are here.

The engines are here.

These approaches are conceptually similar to how humans use pattern recognition, although Machine Learning can find complex patterns that humans might not be able to spot. For instance, we can feed an algorithm millions of images of human cells, and over time, the algorithm may learn to spot the early signs of cancer or disease sooner than human doctors can detect them.

Only a few years ago, the data sets fed into Machine Learning algorithms had to be carefully prepared by conscientious humans. Imagine a well-formed spreadsheet, with very carefully labelled rows and columns and each data type formally defined. (You can revisit that mental image from above of rows of programmers at Orwellian-style desks.) This original, shallow kind of Machine Learning took a long time to prepare and yielded more limited insights, in part because we fallible humans had to perceive and articulate the most important features within the data sets.

A few decades ago, a powerful form of Machine Learning – called **Deep Learning** – was invented. Deep Learning can process 'unstructured data', which means that the data sets don't need predefined formats or manually created labels. Deep Learning can use sorts of digital artefacts like emails, social media posts, documents, videos, and images.

Said another way, Deep Learning lets us find and exploit patterns in unstructured data, which is really an incredible thing.

Deep Learning is one of the major breakthroughs that's enabled the current generation of Generative AI. It lets us train algorithms on books, artwork, and music directly, and we can scale up our data sets to a large size (since humans aren't required to carefully clean and label all of the data), bringing a never-before-seen level of flexibility to the algorithms. And when we say 'large', we mean *really* large. We're nearly unconstrained.

GENERATIVE AI

In a world already full of stuff, Generative AI produces more of it. More stuff for us to consume.

> Generative AI refers to a set of Deep Learning techniques used to generate new, previously unseen artefacts, such as images, videos, or text.

Generative AI produces 'new' artefacts by uncovering and remixing patterns from old, human-created (for now) things. It takes the products of human ingenuity (or of our boredom and idle effort) and somehow makes enough sense of those creations to uncover their underlying grammar;

then it mimics the languages with which they were created to wholly generate new – if technically derivative – artefacts.

For example, a Generative AI algorithm trained on European paintings can learn to recognise the features of the Old Masters' work. Then it can use this information to construct a brand new – but deceptively thematic – image by kludging together pieces of the original patterns. It's like magic but with code.

We already have AI-generated text (like ChatGPT), images (like Midjourney or DALL-E), audio (like WaveNet, which can make spoken language or music), video (like DeepDream), 3D (like GANverse3D, which can generate three-dimensional models of objects, scenes, or people), and gamers (like AlphaGo, which can learn to play complex games at a super-human level). And we've barely begun.

In the near future, we can imagine AI creating more complex artefacts. Anything and everything that humans can create and feed into a computer in some form can be mimicked and blended by Generative AI – faster and with less effort than any human can achieve. And unlike us, it doesn't require a coffee to get started and isn't particularly concerned about whether you say 'thank you' or 'that's brilliant' at the end of the day.

Or to put it yet another way: Generative AI can produce any type of digital artefact that humans can make, as long as the

AI has a large enough data set from which to draw. It's convenient to imagine Generative AI as a black box that's fuelled by data – a mental metaphor that works pretty well.

Data is the lifeblood of Generative AI.

But to delve a bit deeper, it's helpful to note that, similar to an automotive engine, the performance of Generative AI depends on a few factors: the quality and quantity of the 'fuel' (data), design and complexity of the 'engine' (AI model), and computational power available for development.

Algorithms need a vast amount of data. Exactly how much is an evolving art; there seems to be a point of diminishing returns where increasing the amount of data used to train an algorithm begins to have little impact (at least with current model designs). Even so, that point is massive.[1] In addition to size, the quality of the data is crucial. Although techniques can sometimes offset the impact of undersized data sets, no *quantity* of data can compensate for a lack of *quality* (such as diverse and relevant) data.

The performance of a model is also affected by its design – its 'parameters' or internal settings. They're like the knobs and switches that a model uses to make sense of data. Or more concretely, they're mathematical values that articulate the relationships among small pieces of the data, such as the likelihood that any given word ('sweet') will follow another ('bitter') in a Large Language Model. More parameters can make a model more accurate and generalisable, but they also add complexity and computational and memory demands.

For perspective, GPT-4 (OpenAI's language model at the core of ChatGPT) is said to have over 1.7 trillion parameters.[2]

Finally, available computing power is a limiting factor. Training sophisticated Generative AI requires a lot of servers, electricity, and Graphical Processing Units (GPUs), which are advanced electronic circuits originally designed for processing images and videos (hence the name) but that are now used for various complex calculations. This means that hardware, time, and budget all limit how much an algorithm can be trained.

To give a sense of scale, GPT-4 is estimated to have cost $63 million USD in compute-power resources to train it.[3]

The competition for these resources is serious. We've seen international posturing among the USA, Taiwan, and China to secure GPUs.[4] And we've witnessed major scuffles in big-name companies, with critical AI developers quitting in protest over a lack of access to sufficient resources to train their models.[5]

MORE THAN A CHATBOT

With all of the hype around language generation, it may feel as if chatbots are the centre of gravity for Generative AI. But conversational agents (as they prefer to be formally called) are merely one type of Generative AI – one example of what the technology can achieve. There's some value in distinguishing between an instance and a class.

Generative AI is a category of artificial intelligence, similar to the way cargo trucks are a category of automobiles. Chatbots are one class within the larger category of Generative AI, like a panel van is a class of cargo trucks. And ChatGPT – and its fellow name-brand conversationalists such as Bard, Claude, and HuggingChat – are each specific instances of a chatbot, comparable to a specific model of Mercedes-Benz panel van.

Individual instances of a technology may display bias or benefit, and we need to be careful about generalising those idiosyncratic characteristics across an entire class or category of technology.

To extend the automobile analogy, a particular Mercedes-Benz panel van model may appear to have limited leg room and a reputation for being cramped and uncomfortable, but that doesn't mean that all panel vans, or all cargo trucks, or all automobiles are cramped and uncomfortable.[6]

But with AI, it's easy to muddle the discussion.

Conversations about Generative AI, Machine Learning, and Good Old-Fashioned AI are often collapsed into an indistinguishable heap. And it's too easy to conflate the promise and peril of chatbots with the entirety of Generative AI.

We often see a similar imprecision in conversations about social media, where overgeneralised discussions about a particular instance (like Twitter [X] or Facebook) come to encompass the entire notion of online communication platforms.

Of course, a category always has some inherent and defining characteristics. For example, all petrol engines pollute, even the finely tuned and perfected ones, no matter how good the specific instance is. The point is that we have to be careful about how we bound our thinking.

So, what can we say about Generative AI broadly? What features do all Generative AI systems categorically possess?

All classes and instances of Generative AI exhibit **creativity**. (That isn't to say we're necessarily attributing an artistic spark to these algorithms. Rather, we mean 'creativity' in a more sterile and technical sense: the mechanics of creating.) In other words, all Generative AI creates artefacts that have never existed before. It's their *raison d'être*. Each model produces novel content based on learnt patterns, albeit always derivative content, and the degree of artistry and aesthetic appeal of the creations is debatable.

All Generative AI is **data driven**. It relies heavily on data, using large data sets to identify patterns that serve as the foundation for generating content. These data sets are crucial for training the models and establishing the rules they employ in content generation.

Similarly, Generative AI systems have the ability to **improve over time**. Algorithms' performance can be continuously enhanced through iterative feedback loops, fine-tuning, and model optimisation.

Next, it's doubtless that, as an overarching category, Generative AI boasts a **versatile range of potential benefits**. It can be applied across domains and diverse forms of content. It can enhance creativity, support innovation, assist in content creation, and inspire new ideas and possibilities.

Simultaneously, across its many classes and uses, Generative AI raises a number of **ethical concerns**. Questions of ownership and intellectual property rights abound, related to these systems' outputs as well as to ownership of the large data sets used to train them. And like anything humans touch, Generative AI can produce **bias** and discrimination. It can also fuel misinformation, enable bad actors, or generate inappropriate, offensive, or harmful things.

In other words, it's fair to say that, with its immense potential and intricate challenges, Generative AI is a duality. The creative promise it offers can shape a brighter future or cast a malevolent pall over the landscape. The balance between the two rests, in large part, on how we choose to implement it.

We've created engines that don't simply serve us:

They outperform us.

They free us and potentially indenture us.

They feed us and feed off us.

And they may take your job or make you better at it.

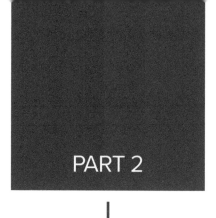

PART 2

Humanum in Machina

AI isn't perfect – because neither are we.

Wade anywhere into the discussion about Generative AI and it's only a short amount of time before someone will mention 'bias'. And rightly so.

We live in an unequal and inequitable world, and the last thing we need is for new technologies to perpetuate or exacerbate historical discrimination. So, it's worth considering the broader nature of why some AI demonstrates bias, how that bias comes about, and whether it's inevitable.

Is bias a transient issue that we need to be aware of and monitor, like a low hum in the background? Is it a recurring issue that we will need to solve, only to have it reinfect us in different ways, so that we'll need to solve it again and again?

Is it a solvable issue at all?

THE TROUBLE WITH TRAINING DATA

Machine Learning gobbles up data like a race car burns gasoline, and the more complex the application – like Deep Learning and Generative AI – the larger and more diverse the data required.

Insufficient or biased data can lead to poor results and inaccurate predictions, and this lies behind much of what we see as bias in outputs today.

Bias enters the system through a number of routes. In some cases, bad actors may feed toxic data as fuel into our engines to pollute them for malicious effects. In other cases, we've starved the engine, giving it too little petrol – too few or insufficiently diverse inputs. Very often, though, the bias is inherent in the contexts in which the AI is deployed – or, at least, in how we (flawed humans) make sense of and digitise those contexts.

For example, a Machine Learning algorithm trained on data from standardised assessments might penalise students from poorer backgrounds because it's learnt the pattern that underprivileged students tend to score lower, then assumes that this historical sociological problem is a reliable feature of the system, an axiom to rely upon and propagate.

We've seen numerous and notable examples of bias in

Machine Learning, like the tendency for early Amazon hiring algorithms to penalise resumes from women[7] or the controversial predictive policing algorithms that disproportionately target minorities.[8] And with Generative AI, even in such carefully controlled applications as ChatGPT and Midjourney, we've seen sexist commentary[9] and racist imagery.[10]

Whilst social attitudes are slowly evolving, the vast majority of our historical written and visual records represent social models that have become outdated.

If you look at earnings data for the last thousand years, those trends will show a bias favouring men because, for much of that time, only men would earn money or own property. And certainly it was mainly the men dictating what the record keepers captured. Even today, when we nominally have HR and legal mechanisms in place to ensure gender parity, few would argue that we truly have it, as the Amazon hiring algorithm disaster demonstrated only a decade ago.

Additionally, the digital culture from which our algorithms learn (the artwork and songs and books on which they're trained) tends to represent a subset of our world's geographical and cultural perspectives. WEIRD – Western, Educated, Industrialised, Rich, and Democratic – cultures are over-represented among the creators and curators of AI. Much less training data exists from literary and cultural artefacts of smaller languages and less-WEIRD groups, meaning they're under-represented and potentially biased against in algorithms.

So, rubbish in, rubbish out.

AI has no emotion. It doesn't 'care' (nor even 'understand') what social disparity is. It simply identifies patterns. If we flawed humans have created patterns of inequity or bias, then the algorithm is merely the mirror through which we view ourselves – a powerful lens through which to self-evaluate and, perhaps, look for clues about how we might evolve.

AN INVISIBLE MIRROR

Whilst Generative AI may speak in English – and several hundred other vernaculars as well as a host of programming languages – no algorithm can truly speak or articulate its thinking.

And neither can we (humans) speak their language. We simply can't crack open the algorithms and read their mechanical thoughts. The language of Generative AI is numbers – an unreadable and impenetrable array of them. Inspired by the workings of human brains, these algorithms rely on artificial neural networks – digital structures that reflect our own minds.

In an artificial neural network, each discrete 'feature' in a data set, such as each word in the English language or even more granular linguistic parts, like word roots and prefixes, is a node. The connections between nodes are analogous to our biological 'synapses', and in artificial neural networks these connections are weighted. The weights reflect the statistical relationships between nodes.

Such relationships are some of those model parameters we discussed in Part 1 – the knobs and switches that make the algorithms work. Formally, these values are stored in something called a co-occurrence matrix – a table of numbers that represents the probability of different words appearing together. In our example, those weights could reflect the probability of a certain word, such as 'bank', appearing in the same sentence as another word, such as 'left' or 'river' or 'money'; or of 'left' appearing with 'right', or 'right' with 'incomprehensible' or 'surreptitious', and so on.

This quickly turns into an explosion of connections.

Of course, language is more complex than a series of two-dimensional relationships. Often, the same word has different meanings and connotations. Context matters too, so additional factors need to be accounted for. ChatGPT employs a co-occurrence matrix with over 12,000 different dimensions to determine the likelihood of 'word co-occurrence'.[11] This means that ChatGPT can take into account a wide range of contextual factors when generating text, including the relationship between the different words as well as their order in a sentence and the general topic. This makes its output more realistic and human-like. However, multiplied out across the thousands by thousands of English words, these numbers exceed our capacity to visualise.

We're unable to interrogate the billions (or often trillions) of mathematical relationships that define Generative AI models. It's an uninterpretable language. To hear it would be akin to listening to the noise of the universe or the buzz of a million silicon dreams.

To further complicate things, the nodes and weights used in artificial neural networks don't explicitly represent meaningful, human-readable concepts (much like some academic papers we've read). These algorithms don't include instructions like 'rate underprivileged children lower' or 'don't hire women'. Instead, they include things like $S(x) = 1 \div (1 + e^{-x})$ concealed within masses of similar mathematical functions.

This is the famous **black box problem** of Machine Learning.

Neither we nor the algorithms can explain the patterns they've learnt. The coherent output they produce emerges from an inconceivable system. It's practically miraculous, when you think about it, and even AI experts are unable to fully explain how it all works. The hatch simply opens and then a song is heard, or a page is printed, or an image is produced.

This is part of the magic of Generative AI: what comes out

of that hatch can't be entirely predictable. Something new is produced each time. But when we look inside, seeking the source of that magic, there's nothing to see but data tokens assembled in statistical gambles.

Consider the earlier example of an algorithm learning to recognise cats from looking at millions of animal pictures. That algorithm can't say, 'Cats have pointy ears' or 'Cats have long whiskers'. These algorithms only 'know' mathematical functions – patterns in the data of the images. And we have no idea what features the algorithm is using to pick cats out of photographs. Even if we unpacked the algorithm and could 'see into' the N-dimensional numerical complexity it produced, we probably wouldn't understand the features it uses or have names for those concepts.

What are the implications of this complexity for our current discussion on bias and error? For one, we can't ask the algorithm how it differentiates cats from other images, and if it makes a mistake – let's say, misidentifies a cabbage for a cat – we can't ask it why.

We can't entirely look into an algorithm's inner workings. We can't kick its tyres or rattle it in frustration.

At best, we can possibly guess that there was some gap in the training data, some quintessential pattern of reality that we didn't sufficiently show to the algorithm. Or perhaps there was some nuanced dimension of probability that we provided too few parameters (too few model knobs and switches) to adequately capture.

Reality has an infinite number of permutations (an infinite variety of cats and cabbages), so there's always a risk that we've missed something.

To solve things, we can try to feed the algorithm more data or allow the model's complexity to expand and then hope for the best. But we'll never really know if we've found the problem or totally solved the issue, except through ongoing trial and error. After all, cats and cabbages may be more difficult to reliably delineate than we first conceive.

Remember that, at some early stage of our lives, we (humans) had to 'learn' to see and to develop the foundational understanding of the world around us, which we now deploy as if it were innate. And to be charitable to the AI Engines, most of us would struggle to explain how we know that a cat is a cat, but at least we have the language to try.

AI engineers are working on this problem from a technological perspective within the nascent field of **Explainable AI**. They're trying to find ways to make the invisible visible, to illuminate the black box a bit more.

But even if they succeed, we still have to overcome the bias inherent in the data or that emerges due to our interactions with an unwitting algorithm.

A MANUAL AEGIS

Even if we can't understand the 'black box' of Machine Learning, surely we can put guardrails on an algorithm's output, filtering out the dross it occasionally produces or placing safeguards on its performance, right?

We can create rules to overcome bias, like the American 'Affirmative Action' programme has done in its attempts to address racial inequalities or the gender quotas that India and Norway have enacted for their leaders.

We can override the algorithm – *homo ex machina.*

And, indeed, this approach is often taken. But before exploring it, let's consider an infamous counter-example, Microsoft Tay – the Boogey Monster and cautionary tale for all chatbots.[12] Tay was launched on Twitter in 2016. The chatbot, which mimicked the language of a nineteen-year-old American girl, functioned pretty well before its release into the wild, but within just a few hours of interacting with internet trolls, Tay learnt to be racist, sexist, and fluent in the Urban Dictionary.

There wasn't necessarily a problem in Tay's underlying model. She wasn't poorly trained or overly constrained in terms of model complexity. Her downfall was poison in the data.

ChatGPT learnt from the 'Lesson of Tay', and its developers established rules, over and above the patterns found in the training data, to ensure its outputs align with certain values, such as helpfulness and harmlessness. To train this, Open AI (the company that makes ChatGPT) hired around forty people to review the chatbot's early outputs and rate its statements for those desirable qualities, gradually fine-tuning the algorithm's performance.[13]

A variety of approaches can be used, whether tuning a model with **Reinforcement Learning** (like the ChatGPT example above) or layering a hand-designed Good Old-Fashioned AI algorithm over Machine Learning output. So, this sort of multi-layered approach seems to have solved our problem, except...

WHO SPOTS BIAS?

Even if we had perfect clarity into the algorithms and were certain of our methods for programming guardrails around them, and even if we had a bias-spotting machine that manually corrected potential anomalies in our patterns, how would we use it?

Which humans could we trust to have the competence and clarity to make things truly safe?

We are biased by nature, even if only through our existing limits of knowledge and constrained experiences of the world. Our brains are also wired to spot patterns that don't

exist or to fixate on preconceptions that shape our subsequent observations. Even our expectations act as a kind of filter, shaping what we perceive and how we apprehend reality. Once we've learnt that something is 'true', we tend to hang onto it with an iron grip, and our minds work hard to fit our observations into our expectations. And on top of this, we live within cultures where dissenting voices can be silenced and where we learn to belong and thrive by conforming.

So, our starting point is that the very humans who are concerned about bias at a structural level may be bad at spotting it in themselves, let alone in others or in systems of systems defined by complex patterns. And even if we finally do spot bias, do we know what to do about it?

It's one thing to have 40 people rate the helpfulness of messages from a novelty chatbot; it's quite another to try to manage predictive policing algorithms or Generative AI that produces new medicinal drug combinations. How do we manage bias when the stakes are higher, more ephemeral, or outright polemical?

For instance, should we tell the predictive policing algorithms to ignore race as a feature of the patterns it learns? That seems like a good start; except it's been tried. Those policing algorithms already exclude race from their training data sets, but other factors, such as socioeconomic background, education, and neighbourhood, end up serving as proxies.

After all, we're addressing systematic biases that are inter-woven into our reality, not merely isolated characteristics we can so easily ignore. That's what brought us to this problem in the first place: the algorithms are identifying real-world patterns – deep, reliable, and repeatable across large sets of examples.

And this returns us to our original question: Who among us has the competence and clarity to define the correct rules that will eliminate bias without tilting the scales in another unbalanced direction or causing other unintended consequences?

Perhaps it would be better for us to simply eschew AI for anything serious. Let it entertain us with clever images or assist us with menial writing but forego its use in weightier situations.

Some regulators in the European Union are advocating for this path, emphasising the need for caution or restricting the use of AI in the most sensitive situations, such as for predictive policing and biometric surveillance.[14] Similarly, the North Atlantic Treaty Organisation (NATO) has adopted 'Principles of Responsible Use', limiting military applica-tions of AI.[15]

Other countries have even banned (what we might consid-er) low-stakes Generative AI because of its perceived bias. For instance, China and Russia have embargoed ChatGPT, claiming it spreads misinformation.[16] What, in our WEIRD cultures, we might say is merely a summary of our world-views, others may perceive as cultural imperialism, and more isolationist nations might even argue that it's a biased distortion (whether or not that argument comes from a place of sincerity).

So, AI – particularly Machine Learning and its derivatives – carries risks, some of which may be challenging for us mere mortals to overcome or to create safeguards against. But perhaps we can exert at least a measure of control through legislation, *if* we can find the right balance, *if* we can under-stand its mechanisms and rippling implications enough to act with wisdom, and *if* we're willing to abide by the Rule of Law, restraining our hubris and exhibiting patience and altruism today to protect our collective future.

The prize for getting this balance right is spectacular. Hopefully, the species that's responsible for the antecedents of those biased data sets will find the capacity to rise to such lofty challenges.

INTERLUDE ON THE COURAGE TO ENGAGE

BY MARC ZAO-SANDERS

The world is fascinated by AI again. The previous 'AI summers' of the '60s and '80s pale in comparison. This time, the breakthrough technology – Large Language Models – has captured the imagination of the general public as well as computer scientists. OpenAI's ChatGPT, in particular, has become the fastest-growing consumer app of all time.

Many aspects of the work conducted by the world's one billion knowledge workers might be carried out by AI. Artists, musicians, writers, editors, coders, marketers, and more all suddenly need to adapt and augment what they bring to the altar of productivity.

Along with this technological progress comes speculation about the future. Opinions reach each end of the spectrum, along with everything in between. Some argue that it's just hype, and the fuss will fade. Others believe that the impact will be cataclysmic, leading to a singularity event that spells the end of our species. Some argue for something in between – that the effect will be massive and life-changing for all of us, similar to other major technological achievements like the wheel, writing, computers, and the internet. Experts also disagree about the speed of this impact, ranging from months to decades. Disagreements are frequently vehement and passionate. This issue has captured the hearts and minds of specialists and laypeople alike.

With important, complex, and controversial issues like this, it's essential to keep a cool head. Hard facts help. Equip yourself with those that seem relevant: How many people are now using Generative AI? What training data does it draw on? How much more data does it need? What tasks can it complete? How well does it complete them? How do we measure that? Which of your colleagues use it? For what purposes? What uses can you, yourself, make of it? What benefits does it bring you, exactly?

A wilful approach also helps in a heated debate. We can choose to be brave and wrong. On the one hand, this means going out on a limb, trying something new, offering a view, and voicing a belief. On the other, it means being open to the possibility that the views we've formed and stated may be wrong. Few of us strike this balance well. We either timidly keep our counsel, refusing to enter the fray, and thereby not contributing to progress. Or we attach ourselves rigidly to one side and become unable to change our position. Technological progress, and indeed progress of any kind, requires us to get involved, to accumulate evidence, and to draw new conclusions as that evidence suggests. This is the scientific method.

Being brave and willing to be wrong are two of the principles on which *Engines of Engagement* has been written. So please read critically. Challenge the assumptions. You may be right, and the authors may be wrong. More importantly, find the courage to join the conversation and influence the evolution of this powerful new technology. ✭

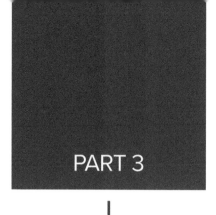

PART 3

|

The Frailty of Intelligence

Generative AI makes us re-examine ourselves from new angles, which is part of the reason it both excites and unsettles us. It calls into question the fundamental things that define us as intelligent, sentient, and human. It forces us to consider new benchmarks of value and to confront some existential assumptions.

Why did we previously associate well-written texts with the truth? What made us think that 'generation' and 'creation' were hallmarks of intellect or that intelligence was one of the gateways to value?

And what, precisely, is **intelligence**?

Our traditional definitions of intelligence tend to focus on problem-solving, an ability to reason, self-awareness, and the ability to conceive of and transfer ideas from one space to another. You could probably legitimately claim that human intelligence is also illustrated by our ability to lie, to cheat, to deceive, to steal in creative ways, and to have invented tax systems of infinite complexity. And arguably our intelligence is also indicated by our ability to play, create, invent, and learn.

But we also tend to define intelligence by what it isn't – by its absence – and we look down on things that lack it.

It's quite a long list. Starting with stones.

Stones, by most people's standards, are not intelligent (unless they're thinking really, really hard). Tulips, similarly, are not intelligent, although they do have the ability to turn their heads to the sun, which beats stones hands down. And it's possible that they can hear and perhaps even communicate in some rudimentary chemical ways.

How about ants? Well, individually they're not strong contenders, but they do seem to achieve quite a lot together. So, maybe not intelligent per se but slightly clever in the collective?

Squirrels? Famously cunning within a narrow and nut-related scope. But nobody thinks that a squirrel will steal their job. So, it's a very limited intellectual capability.

Monkeys? This is trickier. Some of them use tools (one measure of cleverness), and they fight and communicate and care for each other, all of which seems quite human – quite intelligent by our own invented standards. But there's no great concern about monkeys' capacity for collective action to overthrow us nor their ability to replace Shakespeare, no matter how many typewriters they're given.

Babies? Well, Julian's daughter Meadow (aged ten months) once crawled into a corner and was unable to reverse herself out, presumably resigned to the fact that the universe had become smaller and more angular than it used to be. So, obviously not world-shattering intelligence – at least, not yet.

Generative AI? Well, that's the open question. Certainly brilliant in its conception and very handy, but are the algorithms *intelligent?* Or might they be in the future?

WHAT IS INTELLIGENCE?

Scientists measure intelligence in various ways. Many tests involve observations, such as whether a certain species can recognise itself in a mirror or make use of tools. Measures of intelligence might also evaluate how a human or a particularly clever animal performs some challenging task like solving puzzles to reach a delicious treat. There are also standardised tests for the top-tier species, like IQ (which stands for 'intelligence quotient') assessments, neuropsychological evaluations, and achievement exams.

AI can compete on a lot of these, outperforming many talented humans in tests like the Law School Admission Test (LSAT) and Graduate Record Examination (GRE).[17] Recently, algorithms have even earned high marks on Raven's Progressive Matrices exam, an IQ test that presents progressively more challenging questions in such topics as spatial awareness, abstract reasoning, and fluid intelligence.[18]

Do these achievements highlight Generative AI's brilliance, or more accurately, do they call into question our assessments of intelligence or our mute agreement that intelligence is something demonstrable and measurable? Do we conceptualise 'intelligence' as an emergent phenomenon or intrinsic characteristic, or is it more of a value judgement? Does it make us uncomfortable to consider that a stone – that is, silicon – is out-scoring many of us in feats of intellectual prowess?

In a sense, we've engineered the perfect cheat with AI, in much the same way that we've engineered the intelligence tests to begin with, let alone the concept of 'intelligence'. We've built algorithms precisely designed to excel in these bands of cognitive performance. Fortunately, the demarcations of intelligence have arisen from our own collective consciousness, and we also have the power to re-engineer them – to move the goalposts on demand.

But to do so, we must first revisit the question: What do we mean by *intelligence?* Academically, we typically define intelligence (among biological species) as the holistic application of cognition, which includes automatic cognitive processes (like attention and memory), emotions (a necessary component of thinking), and higher-order cognitive skills (executive functions like decision-making). Intelligence emerges from the alloy of advanced cognition, robust emotions, social skills, and self-awareness.

How well do these concepts fit AI? Not especially, as it turns out.

[1]

CONSIDER 'HOLISTIC'. Currently, we rely on 'weak' or 'narrow' AI – algorithms designed to do one thing, like generating text or navigating through traffic. Whilst we can string them together to achieve impressive results, it's unrealistic to expect even the most advanced contemporary applications to excel at every task simultaneously.

Contrast weak AI to 'strong' AI, also known as **Artificial General Intelligence** or AGI. It aims to be able to do everything, all at once – in other words, to be capable of handling the comprehensive range of cognitive tasks seamlessly.

You might have heard debates about this idea. The most sensational argument suggests that AGI could lead to an 'AI Singularity,' a scenario where AI spirals out of control like something out of a dystopian action movie. We currently don't have AGI and may not have it for a long time. The feasibility and potential timeline for realising AGI are hotly debated in the AI community, with arguments ranging from 'it will be invented sometime this decade' to 'it will never happen'.[19] But either way, it's not here yet. So, we can rest easy knowing that humans can still one-up robots in terms of mental adaptability.

We can juggle teleconferences and childcare simultaneously (if not always gracefully) whilst also wayfinding along crowded sidewalks and scanning signs for a suitable place to grab a snack. We've learnt to live in deserts and on the arctic tundra, in shopping malls, and even in space. As a species, we have a healthy regard for our own intelligence and its ability to operate under countless conditions and innovate us out of novel crises. Squirrels do not, and (at least for now) neither does AI.

[2]

AI DEMONSTRATES FRAGMENTS OF SEEMINGLY INTEL-LIGENT BEHAVIOUR, even if it's not (yet) holistic. Is that the same as having bits of intelligence?

Consider the famous '**Chinese room**' thought experiment from philosopher John Searle.[20] Imagine a room with a person inside who doesn't understand Chinese. They're armed with a set of rules, written in English, and a stash of books containing Chinese sentences. When they receive written questions in Chinese from outside the room, they diligently follow the rules to locate the correct responses written in the Chinese books and then hand those answers to a Chinese speaker on the other side of the door. To the person outside, it looks like they're chatting with someone who comprehends Chinese, but the person inside the room is just mechanically following rules without understanding the conversation.

AI is sort of like the hapless fellow in the room. Though capable of performing intricate tasks and producing seemingly intelligent results, it lacks true comprehension. It mimics intelligent behaviour quite convincingly, but does the appearance of intelligence equal the genuine article?

Even the most cutting-edge Generative AI systems still rely on complex rule sets to simulate intelligent thought. These algorithms don't truly comprehend the inputs they receive or outputs they produce. For example, contemporary chatbots might banter convincingly, but they don't understand any of the words. They're just parroting patterns looked up from a billion other texts. That's why some people have called these algorithms '**stochastic parrots**'. ('Stochastic' is a fancy term that certifiably clever people use to mean 'random', and 'parrots', of course, are those chatty avians favoured by pirates in fanciful literature.) In other words, the algorithms appear intelligent, but they're just birdbrains mindlessly following rules.

Not everyone agrees with this sentiment. One counter-argument is that the Chinese room addresses the question of consciousness, not intelligence.[21] Consciousness is a more complex and philosophical phenomenon, involving things like subjective experience and internal mental states.

So perhaps we're reaching too far by pursuing this line of thought in a discussion on intelligence.

If we refocus, we might reasonably argue that an algorithm – or a system comprising many collective algorithms – can be intelligent if it fully mimics all of the cognitive actions associated with intelligence. If it can achieve that, then we've produced the functional equivalent – no need for notions like consciousness or intentionality to enter the discussion.

Before we lose ourselves further down the philosophical rabbit hole, it's worth asking whether AI is capable of such a feat. Is AI capable of functionally replicating the array of mental processes that we call cognition? Can every fragment of intelligent behaviour be mimicked, in some way, by machines?

[3]

WHAT'S THE CATALOGUE OF COGNITION? If we ask an average person what processes underlie intelligence, they might list things like memory and recall, perception, learning, problem-solving, planning, and other higher-level cognitive abilities.

Reasoning.

Deliberate thinking.

We think, therefore we are . . .

...but as neurologist Antonio Damasio famously pointed out, as an amendment to Descartes' truism, emotions are also essential to human intelligence.[22] So, a better axiom might be 'we think *and feel,* therefore we are', amending the checklist to necessarily include emotions along with the other (seemingly more rational) cognitive processes. Through the true story of Elliot, a brain cancer survivor whose frontal lobe was damaged, Damasio demonstrated how higher-order functions like decision-making are intrinsically dependent upon emotional processing.

Perhaps emotion isn't such a shocking criterion for intelligence. After all, even squirrels show a range of feelings from greedy curiosity to anxious self-preservation, all of which temper their decision-making. But squirrels still haven't graduated to the ranks of 'intelligent' species, at least not by conventional scientific standards, despite their often heroic and passionate attempts to steal backyard birdseed. Can AI do any better?

There's a field known as **Affective Computing** that explores how machines interact with human emotions.[23] Using input devices like cameras and microphones as well as noninvasive neurophysiological sensors, AI can recognise real-time emotions with fairly high reliability. Detecting smiles in photos and gauging sentiment in text is even easier. As a result, algorithms are increasingly adept at simulating emotional understanding and parroting back sentimental responses.

Although AI can play the part and say the lines, it's yet to feel joy or despair or to truly empathise with the feelings of another. The algorithms' emotional intelligence is purely simulated, based on mechanical processes that lack the subjective nature of human emotions with their complex interplay of biology, culture, and accumulated lived experiences.

In the quest to imbue AI with more emotional depth, researchers are working on systems that can understand not just the surface expressions of emotion but also the underlying context and motivations. This endeavour extends to developing a genuine **Theory of Mind** in machines.

The Theory of Mind describes our ability to not only perceive emotions in others but also to understand and infer their thoughts, intentions, and beliefs. Humans naturally develop a Theory of Mind as we grow, allowing us to navigate the complex social web of human interactions by anticipating what others are thinking and feeling. It's essentially mind reading. And it's deeply intertwined with our emotional intelligence, enabling us to empathise, cooperate, and form intricate relationships. Whilst AI has made strides in recognising emotions, developing a Theory of Mind in machines, such that algorithms could comprehend and predict the mental states of humans, remains a formidable challenge.

[4]

INTELLIGENCE IS ALSO SOCIAL. Our sense of empathy and

perspective-taking skills – our Theory of Mind – help us communicate and cooperate. We can operate in collectives rather than as disparate individuals, creating and transmitting culture across generations and building on the knowledge and achievements of our ancestors – another defining characteristic of an intelligent species.

So, chimpanzees, dolphins, some clever birds, and maybe even octopuses and fungi are still in the running as 'intelligent' species, but probably not squirrels with their limited social graces. And probably not AI.

AI can simulate social interactions, recognise emotions, and provide human-like responses. It can analyse data to uncover social trends and learn to distinguish behaviours that are socially acceptable in a culture. In collaborative settings, AI can cooperate with humans or other AI agents, and it can replicate seemingly appropriate sentiment in conversations or manufactured videos. However, these manifestations lack the intrinsic qualities that define human social cognition, which forms the basis for our collective achievements and cultural evolution. We build societies, create art, and navigate a cultural tapestry that stems from our unique capacity for emotional connection and shared experience.

Like the Chinese room denizen, AI's social interactions are driven by rules. So, whilst some algorithms may appear social, they're essentially psychopathic inside. But don't worry, they're not (self) aware of the insult.

[5]

THE FINAL CRITERION FOR INTELLIGENCE IS SELF-AWARE-
NESS – the ability to recognise oneself as an individual separate from others and to reflect on one's own mental states
and experiences.

The list of self-aware species includes many usual suspects:
great apes and certain monkeys, dolphins and orcas, the
cleverest birds, elephants and pigs, and (terrifyingly) some
species of ants. But, so far, not AI.

So, to return to the question that started this chapter, 'Is
Generative AI intelligent?' The answer, at least for today,
is 'no' – *if* we agree with the conventional definitions of
intelligence.

But have we aligned those goalposts in the right place? Is
it fair to say that intelligence is something achievable only
after a certain delineation? Does it require the genuine em-
bodiment of emotions and self-awareness, or does functional mimicry at a sufficiently granular level suffice? How much
of 'intelligence' is an emergent phenomenon, and how much
of the notion is more of a value judgement?

Are we really just asking the question:

'Is *my* value diluted by the rise of AI?'

WORSHIPPING THE WORD

We often place words on a pedestal. We give them an intellectual weight and an imbuement of 'truth'. Words voice our innermost hopes or fears, our ideas and uncertainties.

Language gives permanence and expression to our intellectual cores. Through it, we express love, make sense of the human condition, and order our Friday night pizza.

We remember with language.

Spark revolutions by it, and wage battles through it.

It permeates our existence.

In many ways, language forms the conduit between our inner and outer worlds, and it's largely through lenses built of language that we view and interpret the reality around us.

That all sounds rather grand and exciting. So, it's no wonder we've come to venerate vernacular mastery. Literacy – and in particular writing – has long been an established currency of intellect. But now, with an errant thought and a few seconds of spare time, we can generate an AI-crafted essay on nearly any topic. And if today's AI outputs are occasionally lacklustre – only a middling pupil at times – even that degree of coherency is remarkable.

Or is it?

And so we come to question:

What is intelligence?

Should it be defined as a fact or a belief?

And does it matter anyway?

A rigid definition would give us confidence
as to where the race will end, but what if
intelligence isn't one thing but many? Or if
it proves merely a semantic delimitation? Is
intelligence something we value because it's
rare or because we believe it's unique – that
we're unique?

Or will intelligence turn out to be a spectrum
upon which AI – or a tree or a tadpole – may
sit in a line? Possibly ahead of us. Something
commoditised and common? Cheap.

Maybe we'll ultimately peg 'intelligence' to
the ownership of a heart or a wobbly brain?
Or maybe we'll learn to demolish the pedestal
upon which we've placed it.

Is our metric for 'remarkable' appropriately placed? Or to ask a more precise question: How does Generative AI cause us to question our idolisation of well-formed words?

In Part 1, we touched on how Generative AI works, but we'll reiterate a simple explanation. Large language models uncover the relationships between words (or their pieces) and then extensively articulate those interactions as statistical correlations. When you ask a chatbot a question, it doesn't 'understand' your meaning. It's just using its massive mathematical model to parse your input and then predict some reasonable output:

one

word

after

the

next

Generative AI has no sense of reality, writer's block, or self-consciousness. It doesn't ponder the boundaries of intelligence or its place in the wider universe (at least as far as we know). Large language models have never seen the sun or felt the rain. But ChatGPT can write a poem about the weather, and it can describe the feeling of sunlight – along with its scientific principles – more eloquently and thoroughly than you or I might achieve.

But it's all a series (a *very, very* big series) of weighted

functions and probabilities built from patterns found in libraries' worth of human-authored texts. We needed billions of written examples before believably coherent patterns could emerge. But the fact that something has emerged at all – and that these chatbots (despite their flaws) seem so realistic – demonstrates that once enough data has been analysed, hidden patterns can be uncovered, even seemingly inscrutable ones as complex as our conception and articulation of reality.

Many of us had come to view linguistic fluency as a sort of adjunct to intellect – a demonstration of the ability to perceive truths, manifest insights, and reason with wit and wisdom. AI's soulless and thoughtless mastery of language challenges many of our deeply held (even if rarely examined) beliefs.

Today's algorithms navigate language so effortlessly that they cast a shadow on the boundary between syntax and sapience. And like children growing in wisdom, they'll only become more capable in time. Even some AI experts have been unsettled by their capability, with one notable Google engineer attributing sentience to LaMDA, Google's Language Model for Dialogue Applications, thanks to its astonishing linguistic prowess.[24]

It's difficult to accept that language – something so deeply connected to our consciousness and cultures – can be reduced to a mathematical routine. And as we pull at that philosophical string, we quickly realise its connections to our concepts of intelligence, of identity, and perhaps even the nature of reality itself.

Each tied to an unravelling thread.

Could it be that everything we hold dear is susceptible to reductionism, capable of being distilled into mathematical patterns, where statistical frequencies substitute for semantic meaning? If so, that raises another disquieting question: How much of what we esteem as 'general (human) intelligence' is, at its core, merely the biological equivalent of arranging words in intricate patterns learnt through repetition? Were our moments of brilliance genuine, or were they the result of trillions of stochastic imitators, rhythmically drumming on keyboards until the veneer of insight emerged?

THE COIN OF VALUE

As humans – as intelligent persons – we have a distinct identity, consciousness, and spiritual worth. We're set apart from the other species, given a higher status, recognised as 'people' (in both popular culture and law) because of our intelligence.

Since time out of mind, humanity has used the notion of intelligence to drive our concept of personhood and, therefore, of value.

The delineation of persons versus non-persons (biased as such judgements have often been across the arc of history) has been used to justify all manner of oppression and atrocious behaviour. More recently, we've seen the notion of personhood turned towards more positive pursuits, including as a guide to question our treatment of others.

Take the octopus as an example.

As new evidence emerges, we've learnt that some octopuses possess a surprising cleverness and perhaps even an alien intelligence. Many a gourmand would argue that they're no less tasty now that we understand their problem-solving abilities, but their greater intellect gives (some of) us pause.

Have they graduated up the food chain?

Are they potentially nearing 'personhood' status, like the way many of us personify our pet dogs and cats? Is our treatment of octopuses ethical through the lens of personhood?

We like to think we're special, that the mantle of 'personhood' conveys some spark or soul that makes us unique and worthy amongst the species and amongst the stars. The evolutionary rise of mankind through our innate intelligence is a comforting and convenient narrative. But 'special' may be more common than we imagine.

Beyond our solar system, we see that Earth-like planets are potentially not so unique. The universe is a large place, and it seems increasingly unlikely that we're the only ones peering out.

Indeed, it's not inconceivable that we will find traces of life or its building blocks on other 'Earths'. We might find our 'human ingenuity' scattered across the universe. But right here, right now, we feel in control. Our unique intelligence not only allows us to keep animals as pets; it allows us to eat them with a clear conscience.

And as for machines, they're simply tools.

Unthinking and replaceable; certainly not as intelligent – as valuable and irreplaceable – as humanity, but what about apes or octopuses or well-organised ant colonies?

Is there a place within our mental hierarchy of value where we've placed algorithms over anatomy? And what feelings does it evoke when we challenge that ranking? The notion that machines may possess a glimmer of intelligence – and by extension a sliver of personhood – is a paradigmatic shift and most likely one we're not yet ready to make.

Perhaps, the question of AI's intelligence is less about its features, test-taking performance, or even the stories it tells. Rather, to accept AI as intelligent forces us to question the conception of 'intelligence', to recognise it as an engineered notion, and perhaps even to admit that, in some ways, we're not as special as we'd like to believe.

And nobody likes to feel unexceptional.

INTERLUDE ON HUMAN EXCEPTIONALISM
BY DONALD CLARK

In my book *Learning Technologies,*[25] I examine how technologies have been deep generators of culture and progress. Writing, alphabets, printing, broadcast media, computers, the internet, and now AI. Each has augmented, and often replaced, what we do as a species. Yet we still see ourselves as 'exceptional'.

This human exceptionalism − this idea that there's some sort of 'essence' in our species that makes us unique − carries over into our fears about technology. In the third century BCE, Plautus thought the sundial would cause our end by splitting days up into hours. (To be honest, with dull lecture periods in schools and 9–5 jobs, he had a point!) Writing was met with suspicion by Socrates. Printing was denounced by the Catholic Church and Ottoman Empire. Film, radio, and TV were all barraged by naysayers, and the copier was reviled as a destroyer of creativity and copyright.

The internet brought on a new era of revulsion. There were calls to ban Wikipedia (schools and universities blocking perhaps the greatest socially constructed knowledge base our species has ever seen), social media, smartphones, and now AI.

Much of the commentary, especially the ethical noise around Generative AI, betrays a bias towards the northern hemisphere and its institutions. Rather than focus on Generative AI as a great gift for learning and health care, a democratising force and way of reducing inequalities, we get people riding in on their moral high horses, crying about (what I call) the twelve horses of the AI-pocalypse:

1. Plagiarism (cheating)
2. Publishing (copyright)
3. Partisan (language bias)
4. Prejudice (biasses)
5. Provenance (false stuff)
6. Propaganda (duping us)
7. Privacy (data and security)
8. People (dehumanising)
9. Poverty (unemployment)
10. Profiteering (big tech)
11. Planet (energy and emissions)
12. Perish (extinction events)

This isn't to deny that there are ethical issues. But pointing out these risks has become an often lazy pastime for those who typically sit in rich institutions and benefit greatly from *not* using technology. Much of the debate is a heady mixture of confirmation bias, anthropomorphism, and human exceptionalism. Here and elsewhere, an army of ethicists, with no apparent background in either ethics or AI, have flooded forth with very strong opinions about bias, stochastic parrots, hallucinations, and learning.

For instance, academia pounced on Generative AI, not as a force for improving teaching and learning, but as a way to plagiarise in essay writing – perhaps because their business model is based on credentialing. Publishing concerns have focused on copyright, even though nothing is being 'copied'.

My travels in Africa this year have left me hopeful of how Generative AI can give great benefit. I've witnessed first-hand AI capturing and using minority languages, from Afrikaans to Zulu. And for some young Africans, the opportunity to perform work related to labelling and reinforcement learning with Large Language Models (which may be seen as exploitative by some) can be, in countries of high unemployment, a valuable first step into IT.

Another moral high horse is the lack of provenance, in other words the lack of traceability to the underlying sources of information in the models – so that their outputs might be false. There are definitely problems around deepfakes and hallucinations. But the people who panic about AI duping us all are often those who see the 'masses' (and not themselves) as most impressionable. What's more, plug-ins and supplementary AI tools are addressing these problems. Remember, Generative AI is the worst it will ever be. Using ChatGPT 3.5 today is like using Wikipedia circa 2004.

AI isn't a truth machine, but then again, neither are we exceptional when it comes to truth. As if the human mind were free of bias! At least the bias found in AI can be gradually eliminated. That isn't true of the wrongly assumed-to-be-exceptional human brain.

The next horse of the AI-pocalypse is the threat to ourselves as people. Will AI somehow dehumanise us? Of course not; in fact, the opposite is more likely. I can think of no other technology that humanises us more. For instance, with large language models we're able to speak with the accumulated culture of our species – speaking to the whole of ourselves.

But what of our livelihoods? Won't AI put us all out of our jobs and enrich the tech tycoons with our former salaries? Certainly, unemployment may arise initially as AI increases the productivity of today's organisations, but as Nobel Prize–winning economist William Nordhaus has shown, 98% of the economic value created by new technologies flows on to society, making technology invention inherently philanthropic by an order of 50:1. It fuels flourishing innovation through small companies and by enhancing the daily lives of the millions (or billions) who use it.[26]

And for those concerned with the energy and emissions produced by AI, perhaps they should look to other, more serious polluters. Even compared to yesterday's human-driven production of a page of text or digital image, AI requires far less energy. If anything, AI is likely to help us solve the problems of climate change and clean energy.

Lastly, there's the accusation that we'll perish as a species in a mass extinction, destroyed by AI. This is the most extreme form of manufactured human exceptionalism: the millenarianism that we humans seem so fond of. Perhaps, of all things, this sort of apocalyptic end-of-days thinking is the most consistently 'exceptional' thing about us. And if so, we can only hope that AI helps us become a little less 'exceptional'. ✶

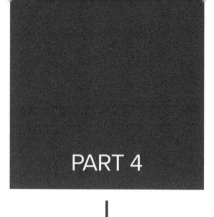

PART 4

Fracture and Evolution

Its proliferation has been so diverse, and barriers to its consumption so low, that we merely have to listen or watch or exist to run into Generative AI in the wild. Even from a fleeting glimpse, we can already begin to see the spirals of possibility. We can envision new uses, new creative methods, new engines of the future, new modes of disruption, new things to be generated and perhaps new views on our own place in this world.

It's reasonable to say that the pace of change is outstripping our ability to understand it, at least in any rational way. As soon as we begin a conversation about, let's say, human-made versus AI-generated prose, the world has already changed – and AI has already out-produced humanity's trove of written artefacts, at least in terms of quantity. We're left standing at the starting line whilst the engines rocket forward.

Performance outstrips strategy.

Action outstrips consideration.

As a result, our human response to the escalating advancement of AI won't be a calm and considered one. We can expect a contentious and combative, litigious and retrospectively legislative road ahead as we fumble our way through this evolution. We're entering this new landscape at a disadvantage and in the clumsiest way possible.

THE RIPPLES OF POSSIBILITY

With innovation, there's always 'the thing' and then the ripples that the thing creates, both across the span of our understanding and over the arc of time.

Take the internal combustion engine as an example. It was developed from a rudimentary mechanism into the highly efficient machines we use today, progressing across time. And ultimately, it's become a forerunner of contemporary electric motors that will soon make it redundant – perhaps in a way similar to how internal combustion engines displaced horses, creating a unique and catalytic link in the chain of history.

Internal combustion engines also radically affected our ways of life. They expanded our patterns of commerce, allowed new forms of trade that, in turn, collided with and collapsed cultures, enabled war to scale, and corroded legacy structures of power that were built on the separation of places in space.

This makes the story of the internal combustion engine not simply one of engineering but rather a narrative of human settlement and exploration, expansion of horizons, and re-interpretation of distance, as well as a story about our desecration of the environment and pollution of the skies.

In other words, the innovation of internal combustion enabled a host of change and achievement, spurred further innovations, and created a rippling array of consequences, both intended and unforeseen. And, although forecasting is always a dubious pursuit, it seems likely that Generative AI has already triggered a similar rippling – one that will reach at least as far as the internal combustion engine's legacy.

THE TRANSFORMATION OF ORGANISATIONS

The impacts of Generative AI on both us and our organisations are probably best understood in three ways. The first way is as a 'change within our systems', the second is as a 'change that fractures our systems', and the third is as an 'emergent capability'.

[1]

CHANGE WITHIN OUR SYSTEMS is characterised by efficiencies and optimisation. Our new AI tools help us gain productivity and expand capability (at both individual and organisational levels), and we can anticipate that they'll add sharp efficiency to generating new ideas and unlocking new opportunities. They'll help us collaborate and make sense of what we discover. They will tell our story for us and extract new stories from the chatter in the shadows.

These are the first impacts to ripple out, and indeed, we're already seeing them. These changes strip cost and complexity out of our existing paradigms of operation – substituting humans with machines, increasing the speed and scale of performance, and likely outstripping legacy infrastructure.

Through the lens of business, this looks like lower headcount, leaner and consistent production, lower costs, and higher revenue (at least until the market rebalances supply and demand). Or to put it another way: short-term profit – perennially a driver of behavioural change in organisations.

But the impacts of AI aren't limited to business: health care, education, travel, entertainment, and even our systems of governance and democracy are wide open to disruption from algorithms.

Health care is a good example. Today, it requires complex and costly infrastructure. It's also dependent on centralised human expertise that tends to be both scarce and expensive, in a knowledge domain that evolves rapidly and, hence, places a heavy burden on individual practitioners to learn the foundations and remain certified over time.

The ripples of Generative AI are lapping at the walls of our hospitals. We already see the rise of the health care chatbot, which rates not only higher for expertise but also for empathy (another frail human trait).

As health care algorithms grow in reliability and availability, they'll bring new capability to our established (and sometimes creaking) systems. Perhaps health care bots will free human experts from routine tasks, easing some of the strain caused by the worldwide nursing shortage and creating more space for medical professionals to dedicate to unique specialisations.

Perhaps we'll simultaneously see an increase in general practitioners and practical nurses, people skilled in a broad range of disciplines but dependent on AI to augment their wide expertise with specialised depth.

Perhaps we'll see a reinvention of the concept of clinics, as the need for physically centralised resources begins to evolve. This might spur the appearance of lighter-weight medical outposts and emergent practice providers. It might even encourage a diaspora of expertise and a corresponding increase in access to high-quality care across the globe, enabled by AI in conjunction with robotics and telemedicine.

Of course, all of this will set in motion subsequent changes to medical billing, schooling and licensing, public health policy, and a hundred other interdependent sectors. It's difficult to envision the path perfectly, except to presage that today's structures will change.

As the health care industry's internal workings evolve, those changes are bound to cascade broadly. That leads us to our second form of change: not only within the boundaries of established systems, but change that remakes those borders.

[**2**]

CHANGE THAT FRACTURES OUR SYSTEMS doesn't simply introduce efficiency into our familiar processes; it disrupts the systems within which that efficiency is held.

For instance, whilst AI may reduce the cost of manufacturing or even expand the delivery of health care, it may also negate the need for the tangible and social structures that currently hold those systems. Or, to put it another way, the changes heralded by AI may lead to abstracted organisations, as those systems increasingly diverge from our current conceptions of them, shifting and disrupting their underlying structures (of organisation, education, power, control, governance, and more) until they can no longer tolerate the dissonance.

The displacement of old systems by iconoclasts, whether internal or (more frequently) external, defines this second category of change: a fracturing and superseding of the structures and stories we thought we knew, a discernible transformation of paradigms and behavioural scripts, a changing of the guard amongst sector authorities and tastemakers.

This isn't so far-fetched. We've seen such upheavals before.

Several decades ago, in the post-Industrial Revolution era (before the Information Age and the rise of AI), industry and power were collected in **Domain-based Organisations**. Those legacy structures of productivity and effect tended to be organised into vertically segmented functions within pyramidal hierarchies, concentrating wealth and power at the top.[27]

Domain-based Organisations grew through the collectivisation of diverse capability (lots of people, brought together and organised), and the use of systems and processes to establish consistency, conformity, and replicability at scale. And all of this typically nested within and on top of a robust physical, and eventually digital, infrastructure.

Through the emergence of the Information Age, we've seen a general shift towards more shared infrastructure, more networked capability, and more outsourcing. What was originally intended to deliver efficiencies within established systems has unintentionally and fundamentally altered those systems, tearing down old infrastructure and inventing new models of operation. We've even seen the rise of infrastructure-free organisations and the **Brand-based Organisation**, which holds market value in its story more than in its concrete, glass, and steel.

To that end, we now have a raft of companies that make

nothing themselves, sit nowhere in particular, and yet trade globally, selling us ideas and stories and, perhaps, even cheap shoes and knock-off coats made elsewhere and by others.

As the balance tipped from the Information Age to the **Social Age**, we saw – and, in fact, are still actively seeing to-day – connections and concepts remodel our organisations.[28] These new structures are undermining old constructs of power and giving rise to new frameworks of citizenship, belief, and belonging – often bereft of any industrial infra-structure or anchored geographical place.

> The *Socially Dynamic Organisation* explores these con-cepts. In that book, Julian examines how technological change led to social, organisational, and societal trans-formations that radically deteriorated our conventional frameworks of power and control, subtly and often sub-versively supplanting them with new constructs driven by connectivity, reputation, trust, and other social cur-rencies. These are the hidden structures that underpin civilisations and shape our behaviours.[29]

The power of Generative AI promises to further accelerate the fragmentation and fracturing characteristic of the Social Age. It does this in part by creating new channels for opti-misation and connection but more radically through the industrialisation of analysis and direction-finding, synthesis and creation, and the integration and exploitation of data. These once-elite capabilities have been widely unlocked, becoming accessible across verticals and businesses of all sizes. This will unquestionably affect our collective frames and foundations.

Who or what is most at risk?

Jobs, clearly, and not just menial ones. Generative AI is impacting graduate jobs too. Jobs that revolve around knowledge, consolidation, interpretation, and planning. Jobs that involve the telling of stories to influence others, to report on activity, or to argue a case. Jobs that require discovery, analysis, and careful intellect. Jobs that involve the efficient management of people, sensitive coaching, and deep expertise. Jobs that require compassion and discretion.

The conventional structures of power, enablement, and employment that held those jobs will also necessarily change. Some may flex, tolerating a 'Type-1 Change' within existing boundaries, such as we explored in the previous section. However, many institutions will resist, holding on to legacy systems until they snap and splinter as new paradigms arise.

We've seen that story play out a thousand times before, as businesses refuse to accept the ripples of change until those waves crash violently against their shores: Kodak and the digital camera. Blockbuster and streaming media. Sears and e-commerce.

To a degree, some FinTech start-ups may be early examples of this change. They operate more like tech start-ups than legacy banking structures, often acting with greater social purpose and possessing enviable levels of agility unobtainable by traditional banks. Regardless of whether any given corporation succeeds or fails, FinTech start-ups collectively demonstrate the fragmentation and vulnerability of the legacy structures in that sector. But FinTech is a known challenger, born during the Social Age but before this most recent revolution in AI.

We can only speculate how Generative AI will accelerate the transformation of the finance sector whilst we simultaneously wonder what other establishments will be displaced by the waves of change. We can already see some of those breakers on the horizon.

Take higher education as an example. Traditional institutions face a significant dilemma, made more onerous when combined with an intolerance for change. Their challenges aren't merely to catch AI-generated essays or to upgrade their delivery platforms with new analytics; rather, these institutions – and their very concepts – are threatened by swells that may reshape the foundations of academia.

AI offers an unprecedented opportunity to reimagine the learning experience. Adaptive learning algorithms can personalise educational journeys, AI virtual tutors can offer instant guidance, and when combined with mobile and

connective technologies, AI allows learning to transcend the limitations of physical classrooms and fixed communities.

All of which is pretty cool.

Yet, the entrenched customs of centuries-old educational models, with their reverence for traditional credentials and the hierarchical dissemination of knowledge, stand as potential barriers.

The temptation to flex, to make conciliatory gestures around the margins, may lead some institutions to superficially integrate AI into their existing structures, only to find themselves outpaced by more agile competitors that have moulded themselves into the new social constructs made possible during this dynamic period.

The waves of AI are already eroding the foundations of the ivory towers of academia as we know them. We explore the evolution of learning and development more fully in the next part of the book. For now, our look at the higher education sector merely serves as an example of 'Type-2 Change' – change that fractures, displaces, and reinvents systems.

But what of the third category of disruption? After innovation comes exploitation: waves of invention, diversification, addition, and convergence.

[3]

EMERGENT CAPABILITY, by its nature, is inherently impossible to forecast. This third form of disruption goes beyond displacement and into rewriting the rules of the game. This might initially manifest as competitors who operate according to neoteric business models, creating new and previously unimagined markets – in other words, businesses that compete not only asymmetrically but also paradigmatically.

From there, the emergent capabilities produce difficult-to-predict secondary and tertiary effects: overturning existing organisational coherence, social conventions, and our familiar ways of life. Indeed, our very notions of work, and of the infrastructure that supports it, of society, of purpose, and of reward, even our structures of habitation and governance may unravel and be wholly supplanted by something new.

In prior waves of innovation, we've witnessed this sort of expansive vicissitude. The internal combustion engine, discussed earlier in the chapter, created those emergent capabilities and compounding ripples. More modern examples are also easy to spot, at least in retrospect:

‣ Netflix and streaming media not only disrupted the entertainment industry but altered how audiences consume creative content, upended media profit models as well as ownership and intellectual property standards, changed the relationship between big data and entertainment, and introduced new genres of story-telling. Arguably, Netflix and its compatriots have even subverted and reinterpreted our mechanisms of global culture.

▸ Ride-sharing apps, like Uber and Lyft, capitalised on the amalgamation of distributed mobile systems, machine learning, and pocket GPS technologies, to not only compete with traditional taxis but to catalyse the gig economy and all of its follow-on implications, such as rewriting employment structures, challenging labour laws, and raising new debates about workers' rights and the nature of work.

▸ The invention of online social networking, through platforms such as MySpace and Facebook, not only revolutionised interpersonal interactions but also redefined how people share information, our perspectives on privacy and digital identity, and the dynamics of power and reputation. They've reshaped societies by disseminating disinformation and empowering echo chambers whilst also creating pathways for collective action and giving voice to hidden communities.

It's worth remembering that all of our social and societal structures are invented; the idea of commuting to work, of earning money, and of being managed, the marketplaces and factories, legal systems and education – it's all made up. It can all be unmade, abstracted from existence, or evolved.

Generative AI may impact some social structures more strongly than others. For instance, its ability to synthesise and produce artefacts in the currencies of scholarship and culture is highly significant. These currencies hold – or perhaps *held* – much raw power. How will opening the gates of access and overloading the channels of consumption affect those dynamics? How will the commoditisation of these artefacts change the way we assign value, or how and what we choose to purchase or spend time with?

The emergent capability enabled through Generative AI will almost certainly lead to new paradigms of health care, finance, education, and manufacturing. Such traditional sectors will undoubtedly be challenged, potentially facing far-reaching structural changes. So, it's an easy bet that at least some of those changes will create emergent ripples.

But talk of change is cheap and, in general, often misplaced.

For example, despite the initial hype, we've yet to see radical disruption ('Type-3 Change' in our parlance) from blockchain technology or the Internet of Things (IoT); instead, we've seen experimentation and gradual integration.

So, who knows where we'll end up? As with many things in life, the real question is less about the destination and more about our journey to it. How will we choose to navigate this sea change? Will we try to buttress established methods and gradually integrate change? Will we try to boldly experiment with volatile but potentially game-changing innovations? Should we throw our arms open and our hands up in the air, or keep our eyes shut tight?

THE METAMORPHOSIS OF ARTISTRY

Generative AI is capable – very capable. Photos (mostly) look real. Essays are (mostly) hard to distinguish from human-written ones. Even music is (mostly) indistinguishable from the popular artists it mimics. It's uncanny in uncomfortable ways.

What does this mean for artistry and for the creators behind the art we enjoy today? Creative artistry has been deeply rooted in society for as long as we've had records. It's how we communicate, how we express our collective souls and our personal identities:

I am a **writer**.

I am an **artist**.

I am a **musician**.

Art speaks to us in ways that live on, long after its originators. But that doesn't mean the pathway of artistic creation and admiration is a smooth one. In fact, even a casual review of history shows that the evolution of art has always

been stormy, with waves of innovation crashing up against the norm: small groups of artists defying convention to try something different, challenging the artistic ideals of the time until they too become the new establishment.

It was ever so, from Picasso offending with his abstract styles, to Warhol mass-producing pop art, to Banksy spraying illegally in the dead of night. Gehry broke architectural norms through his deconstructed works, and rap fractured established creative structures, not to mention underlying power dynamics across the music industry.

New artistic ideas confront current tastes, find new audiences, and then merge back into the mainstream.

Our aesthetic and moral standards shift over time. Graffiti is another recent example – rapidly progressing from anti-establishment protests into a legitimate genre, with many graffiti artists becoming commercial successes (in addition to nocturnal vandals). Tattoos are a mainstream art form now, as is sand sculpture, and – for better or worse – so too is Generative AI.

Contemporary digital artists have powerful robot collaborators that draw on deep knowledge of millions of other artworks to challenge and expand their artistic possibilities. These new tools also open the door of creativity to a wider range of designers. Image-generating AI programs, such as DALL-E, Firefly, Midjourney, and Stable Diffusion, let amateurs paint with words or write their stories from loose fragments.

Art is both commentary and craft. It's both the passion to share a message with the world and the physical ability to create.

For hundreds of years, the great painters had to grind their raw materials and follow closely guarded recipes to concoct pigments. Their profession was as much a craft of building colours as it was the art of applying them to a canvas.

Graphic designers once had to draw with pen and ink, carefully tracing over blue-lined sketches whilst manually separating colours onto different plates and calculating pagination by hand.

In each case, innovation, whether in the form of paint tubes or design software, fomented disruption. Some might argue that Generative AI diverges from these analogies because it's not merely a tool used by artists but can, itself, produce some constructions of art. And whilst there's some validity to that argument, the comparison to paint tubes and digital typesetting is more accurate than we might first perceive.

For those focused solely on the craft, AI threatens to substantially devalue their jobs. For artists imbuing their work with social commentary, novel styles, or unique expression, AI offers itself as a dutiful assistant and creative sparring partner.

What makes a work of art 'real'?

Does the process of its creation matter?

Do artists' effort and sentiment imbue
their creations with value, or is it the
artefact itself that holds worth?

Part of the value imbued in art comes from its novelty and cleverness.

The commonplace, thoughtless, and uninspired are quickly devalued. Just as we've seen a proliferation in terrible design and uncanny photographs thanks to the ease of modern digital design – millions of terrible YouTube movies, distorted Photoshopped images, and soulless corporate slide shows – we've also come to appreciate quality artefacts, which we have more of because of the low barriers to entry.

This can be a good thing...

We have whole generations who can produce songs and tell their stories effortlessly, and Generative AI spreads that access further whilst simultaneously depreciating the manual craft that once was a necessary part of the artefacts' creation.

This can be a good thing...

...unless it erodes the foundations of professional art.

It's fair to wonder whether we've empowered a generation of shallow amateurs and formulaic knock-offs whilst undermining the most original creatives. What happens when there are no new artworks for our robots to learn from? Or when the usurpers of creativity benefit at the expense of the creatives? What happens when a singer's voice is repurposed by a studio, an actor's likeness becomes the property of a corporation, or a designer's style is remixed into imitations by a clickbait farm?

Generative AI is proudly derivative, reproducing mash-ups on demand with no reference to the many artworks that informed them. Each output is clearly unique, but where does the provenance reside, and how do we credit the artists whose original efforts taught the machines?

We have established ways (however imperfect) of understanding authenticity and recognising artistic contributions. Creative works are copyrighted, and creators can expect to receive credit and royalties for their official use as well as for their derivatives, such as a music sample remixed into a new song. We also have a tiered marketplace of value, emphasising original or limited-edition work over mass-produced variations, even if they look or sound similar.

These social constructs are unlikely to survive in their current forms, which will undoubtedly recalibrate the incentives for artists. Even before this latest challenge posed by AI, there's been a rift between artistic creators and the mechanisms for translating their artworks into money.

Streaming services sell access to songs, whilst the original musicians earn only a sliver of those proceeds. Collectors auction artworks for eye-watering amounts whilst the original artists are cut out of the resales. Street artists spray their messages on alley walls, only to see their art extracted and sold in private markets.

We've also seen the industrialisation of art, which cynics might critique as soulless: entertainment agencies mass-producing K-pop bands through formulaic pipelines; major film studios piecing together plots based on snippets of audience screening data; and more recently, the rise of algorithmic manipulations, such as celebrities using bot-based amplification networks to popularise their content.

Do we still value originality? And are we willing to pay for it?

These intellectual property issues and risks to creatives' livelihoods are real, and whilst the proliferation of Generative AI may highlight the struggles more starkly, this is a road we've already travelled – and are actively travelling in many ways.

We continue to shamble down it, unsatisfied and uncertain, questioning and battling with studios and syndicates for the rights of artists whilst, at the same time, streaming and cloning their work. Generative AI is not so much a distinct direction as it is another segment down the same rocky road, and just maybe, the new light cast by Generative AI may help us better see some of the pitfalls along the path.

We don't yet have an answer to this, but if we, as a society, value creativity and authentic artistry, then we need to find ways to support the artists who create it.

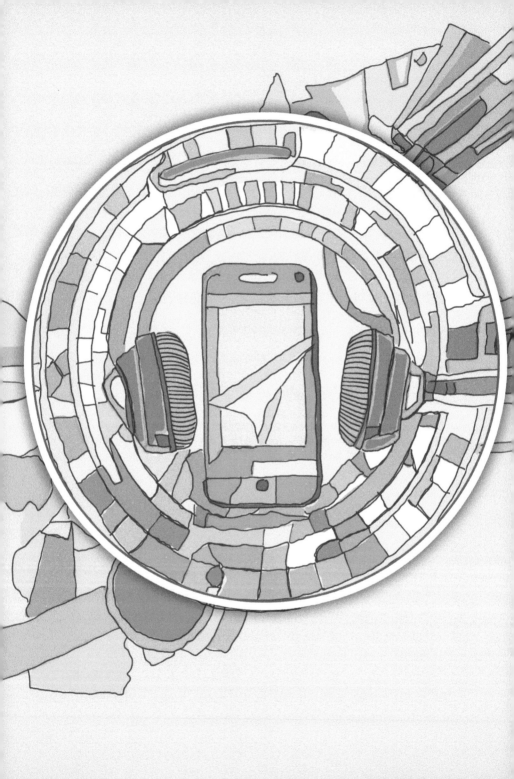

Heraclitus famously observed that no one can step into the same river twice, in part because no one remains the same person over time. Our thoughts and musing, actions and adventures, failures and successes change us. We grow from them. They shape us into our future selves.

As we outsource more experiences to AI – for instance, asking it to generate a sympathy card message or to paint an artistic present for our mother's birthday – it's not only the (potentially unwitting) recipient who's affected. We, the creators, have missed out on the experience of examining our feelings as we write. Or of reminiscing about time with mom as we sketch. Or of the frustration of fumbling a brush-stroke and the small lessons in patience and self-growth such moments build.

As millions of those modest and unassuming moments are replaced with automation – as artefacts once made by our own hands and minds are instead effortlessly produced with a thoughtless push of a button – how does that change us (or neglect to change us) as individuals?

Collectively, as social beings, as we strip out more and more of these micro-experiences, how does it change our interactions and expectations, scripts and stories, tolerances and values? By removing so much friction, and consequently so much experience, from the act of creation we may be poorer in subtle ways that ripple through our thoughts and behaviours, into our tribes and communities, and perhaps even into our structures of society as a whole.

THE DECADENCE
OF CULTURE

Art and culture are symbiotic. Culture is captured in, and reflected by, the artefacts we create, and those artefacts impel the zeitgeist, the spirit of an age.

Art reflects life reflects art.

Naturally, as the creation and dissemination of art (in all of its many forms) becomes more accessible, there's a reciprocal effect on culture. Even before the rapid proliferation of Generative AI, we'd already begun to see the bellwether of this phenomenon:

> The half-life of culture
> is contracting.

In ages prior, it took decades, if not generations, for new styles of art, music, and literature to accrete and emerge. Culture built slowly, and with each new masterpiece and movement, we collectively gained new perspectives. Artists discovered new depths of inspiration, and gradually – often sprouting from the time-worn remnants of prior iterations – new cycles of culture blossomed.

In our media-dense Information Age world, we already find that new creations (if they prove to be popular) only hold our collective attention for moments, until toppled by the new, and then the newer, in an accelerating and ever-shortening life cycle of tropes and trends.

As the revolutions of culture grow more streamlined, and we spiral ever faster, we lose something in their experience. We lose the contemplation and settling-in of ideas that we once found in the lag. This is not simply a nostalgic perspective. Multiple forces of the Social Age act upon this dynamic – our radical connectivity, rise of community, rebalancing of power, and value ascribed to authentic voices, all streamline the mechanisms of culture.

AI shortcuts things even further.

Generative AI accelerates creative production and opens the gates of artistry to more creatives, each of whom can produce new works with little time and, often, less effort.

Millions of budding artists can explore a style, try infinite perturbations, eventually stumble upon something new, and perhaps even fleetingly popular, and then just as easily discard that innovation for the next one – placing small value on the invention and spending little time considering it. This isn't necessarily bad in itself, but it's clearly an evolving feature in the mechanisms of culture.

Not only do we shortcut the arduous perfection of process but also the time scales of creativity. As Generative AI and other digital tools hasten our cycles of creation, diffusion, fragmentation, and radical iteration, how does this change our relationships with artistic expression and its cultural significance?

We're already voracious in our capacity to consume media and swift in our tendency to tire of yesterday's creations. We're growing increasingly inured to and dependent on novelty, and our brains are already wired to imbue value into scarcity and, in turn, to devalue the commonplace.

Overabundance shortens our attention spans and diminishes our depth of engagement, potentially reducing the emotional and intellectual impact of artefacts and challenging our sense of cultural memory. The traditional markers of value, such as rarity and exclusivity, are correspondingly declining – transforming the ways we assign importance to different artworks.

The wheel spins faster and faster.

Though each resulting thread seems to matter less and less.

We have some influence in how this adventure plays out, even if only in our own minds. Do we dedicate our cultural selves to the global, AI-enabled artefacts that flood our feeds? Do we doom-scroll eternally and mindlessly through fleeting content? Or do we intentionally slow things down by seeking local retro-artefacts and practising mindful consumption?

Will it all come out in the wash?

Possibly. But so too we may decline. We may become less, even as we create more.

There's no preordained condition that things always get better or progress in an upward trend. There's equally no reason for 'different' to mean 'worse'. Either way, sometimes we have to steer.

THE DECAY OF OUR TRUTH

If you've managed to avoid sending your life savings to a Nigerian Prince and declined to procure assorted cure-all from various latter-day shamans, then the chances are your BS filters are working just fine – or at least they were, up until now.

Over the years, we've learnt the signs of spam emails: poor graphics, odd addresses, and linguistic mistakes. We grew adept at spotting clickbait articles, with their formulaic headlines. Usually, we could discern 'fake news' videos too, with their poor editing and clear distortions, and most of us would think twice before handing over our banking details to a cold caller, even if they claimed to be a long-lost cousin.

The flip side was also true. We had developed filters to distinguish the genuine: well-written and personalised messages, high-definition videos, and professional-looking photos released by established news outlets.

But our filters are clogging.

The Engines of Innovation have, in part, become Engines of Distortion, warping our reality in both unintended and insidious ways. Generative AI introduces countless new ways to erode our sense of what's real and true. It even makes us question the extent to which the distinction between reality and fiction is still valid.

Our lenses lie shattered. Our perception of truth is in decay.

The danger extends beyond fringe scammers and industrial deception. Today, we're concerned about the robustness of democracy and the reliability of global communication.

We had come to trust the written word, but now we've learnt to un-trust it. We once believed the reality captured in photographs, but now we doubt our own eyes. Even video and voice have become things that can be conjured from dust, a sophisticated – and yet readily made – digital deception. As a result, suspicion has been injected into nearly every channel, and we often respond to new information with incredulity, sometimes never budging from that starting line, regardless of evidence.

Because simply 'seeing' is no longer 'believing'.

This is more than the mainstream erosion of truth; there's also a growing cynicism about the concept of 'truth' at all. As humans, our brains are inclined to disengage from such complexity. Abundant competing narratives, along with the hyper-awareness and hyper-criticality we need to navigate them, discourage us from searching for the signal in the noise. We question and doubt, then grow tired, and eschew the whole exercise.

As truth distorts, trust becomes more fragile. We grow sceptical of signals from outside our immediate control.

Our worldviews narrow.

We disconnect and disbelieve.

Things that we venerate may fall away as that belief erodes.

'Truth' is a tricky word. We use it interchangeably to describe that which is universal and that which is individual, that which is quantifiable and that which we simply believe. That may seem anathema to those who seek to surface 'a' truth or 'the' truth. And certainly, there are more universal principles: gravity is a 'truth'. But so too is my sense of belonging.

Truth can be contextual. Scientific 'truth' – the kind we give Nobel prizes for – may be less mutable, but the grubby and fractured 'truth' that we each construct in our minds and amongst our tribes is subjective. We hold those truths close to our hearts and, when challenged, often cling to them more tightly. We fight to the death for those truths.

Individually, we tend to believe that others are more impressionable, more likely to be deceived than we ourselves are. But perhaps the nature of deception is changing as we're immersed in a sea of new 'truths' with infinite stories acting upon us. The proliferation of generated 'alternative truths' may push us into inhabiting landscapes of partitioned belief, and perhaps we risk abandoning the concept of collective truth altogether.

Or maybe we will be just fine. We're not trying to be doomsayers but pragmatists. The practical path requires us to be clear-eyed about the mechanisms of change that act upon us – not to draw a conclusion (or construct a rigid new 'truth' about it) but neither to naively trust that everything will work out on its own.

To find our way through the noise, we'll need to develop new filters. We'll need new ways of navigating information, new tools for building trust, and new mechanisms for constructing shared knowledge and learning about the larger world.

Ironically, we'll need to rely on the Engines – those same innovations that antagonise the concept of truth – to prepare and equip us for traversing this 'post-truth' landscape.

INTERLUDE ON SYSTEMS OF SYSTEMS

BY MARK OEHLERT

There is an old joke that goes: 'I don't know who invented water, but I bet it wasn't fish'. The implication being that we tend to ignore those pieces of our environment that are both so present and yet somehow manage to fade into the background.

What's that got to do with Generative AI and the changes it's bringing to almost everything? Awareness of those invisible but crucial elements of our operating environment will tell us, almost like tectonic plates, where there will be collisions between the old and the new. Consider this list: copyright, double-entry accounting, job descriptions, performance reviews, and assessments. To one degree or another, all those systems or avatars of systems will limit, impact, or clash with Generative AI's rollout.

The copyright clash has already begun. There have been lawsuits by artists against MidJourney, Stable Diffusion, and DALL-E alleging that they've trained those models to emulate an artist's style without their permission or compensation. There's already a start-up, Kudurru, that allows artists to either block AI-based Internet Protocol addresses or actually 'poison' the AI requests by sending back a different image than the one requested. There are comparable lawsuits on the text side as well. These battles will have to be fought and decided as we go forward.

Let's say you deploy Generative AI in your organisation. Your organisation has a contract with OpenAI that lets your employees build GPTs, powerful and customised versions of the ChatGPT bot which individuals and organisation can develop for specific uses.

So, imagine that your organisation has some of these bots for internal use. Did you actually hire anyone to do that? Is that anyone's job description? How will you rate and assess their work and their value to the organisation? If these folks begin deploying amazing GPTs that save the organisation significant amounts of money, how do you account for that person's value to the company? According to double-entry bookkeeping, you can only account for employees as costs, liabilities.

One final thought, if Generative AI can automate so much of what's been our activity within organisations, then how will our value be gauged? How will we think about moving people's work up the value chain so that Generative AI isn't just eating our organisations from the bottom up?

There is a site, *There's an AI for That*, that includes a Job Impact Index. The Index looks at the percentage of a job that could be impacted by AI. The CEO has a 91% impact index focusing mainly on team management and performance reviews. Have we begun to think about that level of impact from the top down and how we'll have to be aware of, and work to adapt, our systems to that impact? This book will help. ★

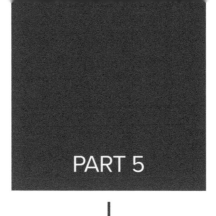

PART 5

In Dialogue with Learning

From the moment we're born, staring up at the hazy faces of our parents, we're recognising patterns and trying to make sense of the world around us.

Our brains are amazingly malleable, and the more diverse and varied the experiences we have, the more agile and powerful our brains become. We're able to navigate new, previously uncharted situations by drawing on the fragments of knowledge and lived experience we've collected over our lifetimes.

Learning is the process of experiencing and growing, and then reasoning and engaging based on those encounters. It's quintessential to the human condition. It's sort of our superpower.

Machine Learning has surprising parallels to our own (human) learning processes, with algorithms essentially training themselves by observing and making sense of many millions of digital experiences. Thanks to this, Machine Learning and its progeny, Deep Learning and Generative AI, have the power to fundamentally reshape how we, as humans, engage with learning – in schools and vocational centres and across its many variegated forms and facets. We're only just beginning to understand what this might look like ...

LENSES OF LEARNING

Learning takes place everywhere, all the time. If you walk down an unfamiliar hallway and stub your toe on a well-camouflaged door stop, you've received a memorable lesson. And in the future, you'll probably adjust your behaviour to avoid that obstacle – indicating that you've learned.

We learn on the job, in our communities, from our mentors and colleagues, and of course, within formally defined structures. Most of us initially experienced formal education in childhood, likely in a classroom with desks lined up in rows, facing towards a teacher who stands in front of a chalkboard or, perhaps nowadays, a smart board.

This image of a 'traditional' classroom is often called the 'Industrial Age' learning paradigm, and it traces its origin to the eighteenth century Prussian school, a ground-breaking innovation for its time. These primary schools fostered widespread literacy and numeracy among both boys and girls in a time before mass education had become commonplace. Prussian schools emphasised discipline, obedience, and respect for authority. Students were expected to conform to rules, and teachers primarily used drill-and-practice methods, instructing through repetitive rote learning.

In the twentieth century, as education and psychological theory advanced, so too did our understanding of pedagogy (the science of teaching). Constructivism replaced the old Behaviourism paradigms, signalling a shift from rote learning to internal knowledge construction, and more active instructional methods were introduced – albeit into classrooms that still largely resembled those old Prussian schools. So, even though we had updated our curricula to align with modern sensibilities, we were still deploying them within Industrial Age models.

As we neared the twenty-first century, the World Wide Web opened widespread access to information, and we grew more dubious of the Prussian model, deeming it inadequate for the evolving educational and informational landscape. It seemed too simplistic in an era where information was increasingly abundant and accessible.

The proliferation of internet access, search engines, and social media makes it effortless to retrieve books and articles, step-by-step instructions, and instructional videos. In many ways, we can even substitute internet artefacts for our lower-level cognitive skills. We no longer need to remember simple facts; we can look them up with a few keystrokes. We don't need to understand the underlying principles to solve a problem; we can ask online communities to 'Explain Like I'm Five'.

These new capabilities and their effects on our learning and cognition triggered another recalibration. Education professionals began to emphasise 'Information Age Learning' and 'Twenty-First Century Competencies'. Teachers were encouraged to nurture their students' critical thinking, analysis, and synthesis skills and to use more holistic and adaptable approaches. And new theoretical paradigms about the Social Age and **Connectivist** learning emerged. These frameworks emphasise distributed cognition, networked expertise, social learning, and the synthesis of fractured information. They recognise that sense-making is both an internal and a collective capability.

Connectivism sees learning as a social process – not something that's solely internal and individual but something distributed and dynamic. Connectivism focuses on growing learners' capability to manoeuvre through the web of sources and communities scattered throughout our sociotechnical world. It suggests that learners should focus on learning how to navigate information and cultivate networks of resources and peers. It encourages the development of such skills as digital literacy, network literacy, and the ability to critically sense-make from disparate (and sometimes questionable) sources.

Similarly, the notion of **social learning** in the Social Age frames learning as the construction and sharing of 'meaning' within and between individuals and across organisations.[30] Meaning-making goes beyond the transfer of information, the production of knowledge, and even the individual – becoming an emergent narrative or diverse narratives that arise from a community. 'Meaning' acts both as the legacy (output) of learning as well as a schema for the community's ongoing sense-making: perceiving, decision-making, and action all take place within a fluid complexity of ideas, identities, and interpretations, all of which individuals and organisations must learn to navigate.

Contemporary AI shifts our relationship with knowledge further.

Although the Social Age and Connectivist capabilities are likely to remain indispensable, just as surely they – and the old Prussian-inspired educational frameworks in which they were developed – will no longer be sufficient.

STUMBLING TOWARDS EXPERTISE

Deep Learning algorithms surface complex patterns for our intellectual consumption. Narrative and dialogic tools slide gracefully into our natural mechanisms for curiosity and exploration. And in its many everyday uses, Generative

AI neatly replicates many aspects of higher-level human cognition. We can not only find information almost instantaneously, but now we can also ask for help summarising it, analysing it relative to other concepts, applying it to our unique situations, and even evaluating what and why certain concepts are relevant.

All of this introduces considerable uncertainty into the landscape of learning, particularly formal education, training, and testing.

We could argue that pretty much everything is on the table right now: the nature and role of teaching, the ownership and use of educational materials, the structure of our educational systems, the ethics and mechanisms of assessment, the impact of a growing digital divide, and our established model of education, performance, and the cultivation of capability. These new tools even challenge our perspectives on what 'capability' is as well as how and where it's held by individuals and institutions.

For starters, let's consider foundational learning.

In the old model, someone might 'stumble towards expertise', grinding through the low-level, often just-better-than busywork tasks, potentially for years. In primary school they might have months of grammar study and spelling lessons over many semesters, hundreds of poorly written secondary school essays, and eventually blogs, low-risk articles, and published works.

A few of these workers (in our anecdote, these budding professional writers) would gradually gain the insights that would bring them to the attention of a boss or mentor, who would elevate them to sink-or-swim at the next level of performance. And, gradually, the cream would (sometimes) rise (some of the way) to the top, as individuals constructed their internal infrastructures of capability, bit by bit from the bottom up.

With spell-check and grammar plug-ins – let alone Generative AI to craft basic essays – many of these early education and entry-level tasks are less important, if not entirely redundant. However, the core capacities learnt through those experiences remain essential, such as developing persistence, good judgement, and a sense of self-awareness as well as an intuitive understanding of the components of good writing like pacing, clarity, and voice.

Similar stories could be told for digital artists, instructional designers, filmmakers, attorneys, financial advisors, software developers, and of many more professions. Across disciplines, the low-level grind that novices plough through historically developed the mindsets and capabilities that eventually became the foundations of their expertise.

But no longer.

So, how do we adjust our educational models to continue

developing these expert capabilities – things like higher-level competencies, nuanced contextual understanding, and automaticity – when the incentives of slogging through the lower levels have all but disappeared? How do we help novices mature their knowledge and skills when the foundational components on which they're built can be accomplished effortlessly by digital tools?

We've seen similar scenarios before.

When calculators were introduced to education, people feared that students would no longer know how to do maths if they weren't forced to perform four-digit multiplication in their heads. In retrospect, we can recognise that mathematics involves so much more than basic arithmetic and that digital aids have actually accelerated the field. Today, mathematicians cohabit with technology, learning to use graphing calculators at an early age, applying specialised software in their senior projects, and building their own macros and applications at work.

Skills like estimation, data literacy, and probabilistic thinking have grown in importance, not only among professional mathematicians but broadly. Yesterday's pre-digital experts developed such capabilities intuitively as they worked their way through mental algebra and the drudgery of lower-order mathematics. Today, we need to conscientiously develop higher-level numeracy skills in students, and we've successfully built curricula and pedagogies to support that task.

It's tempting to believe that Generative AI will follow a similar course, but despite surface similarities between the introduction of calculators and our current situation, the two cases may not be so analogous.

Digital tools fit neatly into the repertoire of mathematics; they're close cousins after all. And digital tools proliferated gradually as the Information Age developed. In contrast, the introduction of Generative AI has been both widespread and sudden, shaking the foundations of nearly every academic discipline in an instant.

In less than a year, almost every commercial productivity tool has incorporated some variation of these AI capabilities. Generative AI algorithms are already quietly nudging and improving our work. The breadth and speed of change implies that this is unlikely to be the gradual evolution we saw with calculators and computerised spreadsheets. It's liable to be the system-shattering kind that breaks established paradigms and sends unpredictable ripples across sectors, sparking opportunity and seeding innovation.

Education and training professionals are at a crossroads, facing the choice of defending a questionable status quo or walking down an uncertain – but likely empowering – algorithm-lined path.

EMERGING ENGINES OF LEARNING

To be fair, AI is already in education, especially Good Old-Fashioned AI and Machine Learning. Learners are graded and ranked with AI. Universities distribute funding based on AI predictions or identify at-risk applicants thanks to algorithms. Students use AI-powered platforms to practise for exams and to 'cheat' on their homework, whilst proctors use it to flag misconduct and wrangle for academic integrity. And beyond enterprise software (such as the student information systems and e-learning platforms that schools and training centres use), there's also a growing market of direct-to-consumer EdTech applications that incorporate AI.

Free of the centuries-old dogma and institutional inertia that limit formal academic organisations, EdTech companies have already exploited the cracks opening within the dynastic structures of education. The fissures are only widening, and through those channels, EdTech companies are starting to flood the landscape with Generative AI, triggering paradigmatic change with or without the blessing of legacy institutions.

This new era of learning by, with, and through Generative AI will need new models of pedagogy and scaffolded self-development, new tools for assessment, new competencies to promote, and new methodologies of synthesis and collaboration.

Let's consider some of these emerging Engines of Learning and the ripples of change they'll likely provoke.

[1]

Accelerating a growing trend, education and training will likely move away from linear frameworks in which learning experiences are organised into separate subjects and se-quential blocks. We'll replace them with web-like models – more of an **ecosystem**, in which different chunks of learning are generated, compiled, and delivered based on individuals' needs, rather than a long road that we all travel down.

This approach relies on **personalisation** enabled by AI.

Many of the smarter EdTech platforms already offer var-iations of personalisation, albeit in silos. For instance, a language-learning app might use AI to evaluate how well a learner is progressing and subsequently offer tailored feed-back, hints, and content sequencing. Until recently, this kind of adaptive learning was a rarefied offering, the kind of unique value proposition that propelled apps such as Babbel and Duolingo into massive market shares. Today, it's table stakes.

Soon, we'll expect any decent learning platform to include personalisation – not merely content filtering (which recom-mends 'next up' learning activities) or simple decision trees (which give pre-made feedback based on specific errors) but wholesale generation of new media and learning paths based on individual needs.

Personalised (also called 'adaptive') learning is a well-developed science, originating around 1960 from the intelligent tutoring field. Historically, personalised learning applications were time-consuming to create and narrow in scope. Nonetheless, well-designed systems have demonstrated powerful results, with boosts to learning outcomes showing, on average, medium to large effects.[31] The best systems show extreme benefits. For example, one famous intelligent tutor trained novices to become IT technicians. It produced effect sizes up to 3–4σ (which you can think of as 3–4 letter grades) better than traditional vocational education, and learners who used the tutor outperformed seasoned professionals after only 16 weeks of training.[32] This was achieved years prior to the current wave of AI innovation, which implies that the hyper-contextualisation and personalisation achievable through Generative AI is likely to produce even more astounding results.

Generative AI empowers the ultimate personalisation: my questions and curriculum built for me, and yours built for you. For example, at the lower levels of learning a new language, someone might rehearse useful words or phrases, repeating the ones they struggle with more frequently and getting customised feedback on pronunciation errors. At the mid- to upper-levels, a learner might immerse themselves in books, movies, and conversations generated on demand by AI to precisely match their level, interests, and goals. And when it comes to testing and credentials, a learner's digital portfolio – rather than a single high-stakes test – might become the evidence of their competence, thanks to AI-enabled analysis of their body of work.

[2]

With the right prompts, Generative AI can produce thousands of variants of a learning activity. It streamlines the administrative burden of designing and developing almost every type of **content**: lesson plans, articles, exercises, tests, rubrics, competency frameworks, virtual environments, and even entire digital courses.

The knock-on effects from this are difficult to fully predict. At a purely mechanical level, the costs of production will be significantly reduced (free textbooks, anyone?). From an educator's perspective, there's no longer a significant cost to personalised learning. Why give every student the same coursework when we can generate unique tests and homework for everyone?

Companies that make their living licensing content or creating exams are scrambling to adapt their workflows to include AI. This is probably a terrifying time for traditional publishers who find themselves selling a rapidly devaluing resource whilst struggling against the inertia of their anterior business models.

Widespread access to cost-efficient AI-driven **simulations** and virtual environments will revolutionise practical and hands-on learning. For instance, medical students can practise surgeries in a virtual operating room, experiencing an infinite number of scenarios invented to target their particular learning needs or to help them prepare for forthcoming procedures. Engineering students can test complex structures in immersive digital environments, making mistakes safely and iterating their designs with the help of a Generative AI companion. Within and beyond educational settings, virtual environments powered by Generative AI will let us manipulate ideas, experience new ways of seeing and knowing, and prototype rapidly. Such capabilities not only accelerate the pace of invention; their use will soon become compulsory for knowledge workers in certain fields, assuming they want to be professionally competitive.

[3]

As the pace of advancement continues to accelerate, it will change – and, in fact, it already is changing – the job market. AI and automation, combined with societal shifts such as diversifying careers, longer lifespans, and increasing industrial complexity are reshaping the requirements for employment, and not just today or tomorrow but continuously, necessitating ongoing development for employees across many disciplines to remain competitive.

To keep pace, we'll need to engage in **lifelong learning** – developing new knowledge and skills from childhood through retirement (whatever 'retirement' will come to mean). Or as some at Harvard have dubbed the concept, we'll need a '60-Year Curriculum' – a scaffold for learning throughout our working lives.[33]

The currency of education will likely shift away from traditional degrees and towards a more dynamic approach, where individuals select from a buffet of learning options and use tools like **micro-credentials** and competency-based 'learner wallets' to validate their capabilities. The landscape of learning may fragment as individual paths and divergent narratives replace mass education models.

We can envision **dedicated AI tutors** who help us wayfind through this new terrain. These digital mentors, perhaps given to us in childhood, will gradually 'learn' from their experiences (building efficacy over time) just as we learn from them, so that we grow symbiotically. They can become our perfect advisors – always available, with flawless memory of our preferences and objectives, never judgemental, and versed in such methods as Socratic questioning, role-play, and reflective feedback.

These learning aides won't simply accelerate knowledge acquisition along established routes; they'll also change the nature of learning, making it social, even when solitary. When we're 'in dialogue' with these algorithms, we're using

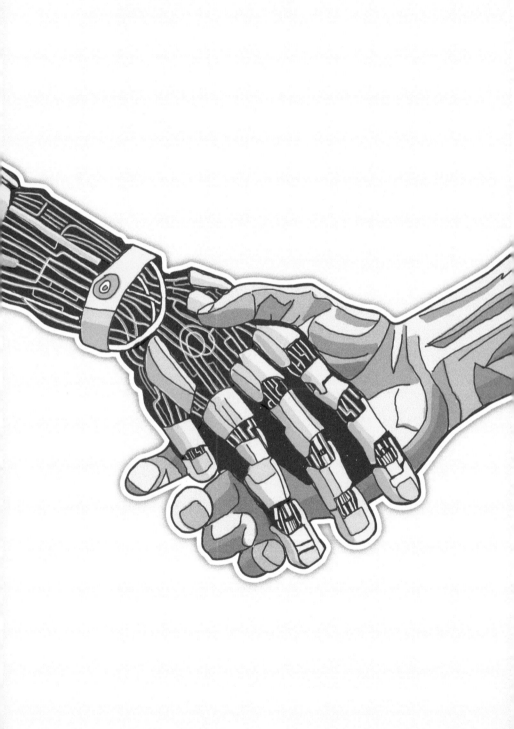

some of the same mechanisms of enquiry and community as when we dialogue with each other. They can help us grow our meta-cognition, critically examine our thinking, and even cultivate our empathy.

In addition to AI 'others', we can similarly imagine AI replications of ourselves. **Digital twins** can become a mirror through which we examine ourselves and explore the downstream impacts of different decisions on our capabilities, well-being, and achievements – simulacra of a million possible lives.

Combined with an ecosystem of personalised learning resources, these capabilities are certain to have a profound influence on not only *how* we learn but also the social and physical structures within which we do so. Already, our shared concepts of 'education' and 'work' – as bounded formal structures within fixed locations and schedules – are eroding. New models of access, distribution, and permeability are leading to a disaggregation of expertise as well as broader patterns of change.

In his exploration of the Social Age, Julian has hypothesised that we'll see an emergence of **New Guilds**: essentially, new social structures that form the backbone of careers. These patchwork communities will hold information and expertise, power and reputation – subverting the hierarchical model where organisations 'own' performance and universities 'own' knowledge. To some extent, we already see this shift in fields such as cybersecurity, which would be almost impossible to perform inside rigid organisational borders or without the aid of interconnected, capable communities of practice.

The concept of New Guilds typifies the patterns of change that, at the broadest level, will come to affect the fundamental structures of society – those mechanisms of power, security, profit, and law that form the latticework in which we live.

If these predictions seem to overreach, consider that once individuals are entirely unmoored from the confines of formal education and are incited by pervasive developmental opportunities, there will surely be wide and numerous repercussions. The legacy contexts of learning, traditional sources of knowledge, and one-time oligarchs of academic authority are wavering at the precipice of disruption.

[4]

One thing unlikely to change is our need for **assessment**, although the *ways* we collect that data as well as *what* we collect and *how* we use it are undoubtedly evolving.

'Assessment' is so much more than tests, grades, and credentials. In the purest sense, 'assessment' refers to the documentation of characteristics, context, or competence, typically in some kind of quantifiable way, even if the target is qualitative or hidden. However, given our experiences in formal education, many of us have come to associate it with bubble-sheet tests and red-inked exams – dismally poor callipers of capability.

Still, we've tried. And educators and psychometricians have significantly matured the field over the years. For instance, standardised tests (such as the GRE and Cisco Certification Exams), as well as some personalised learning platforms and employee assessment programs, have used both Good Old-Fashioned AI and Machine Learning for a while. And for over fifty years, **Computerised Adaptive Testing**, where the difficulty of each subsequent question is adjusted based on the test-taker's performance, has used AI.[34] Despite these applications, AI's use in assessment has been relatively constrained until recently, in part because of our somewhat limited approaches to the measurement and evaluation of learning.

Traditionally, we've largely relied on explicit and summative forms of assessment: in other words, tests that are separated from performance as well as intersecting topics, tests that happen at the end of some milestone (like the end of a course or a predefined recertification period), and tests that occur in a bounded moment in time. High-stakes testing is one example.

Formative tests, sometimes called 'tests *for* learning' (in contrast to summative 'tests *of* learning'), are also used. Formative tests are generally small, in-progress checks meant to inform an instructor or a computerised system, or to help learners gauge their own progress. Formative assessments might look like homework problems, low-stakes quizzes, or in-app activities.

Generative AI is well-suited to support both of these conventional forms of testing. Generative algorithms can create countless iterations of similar questions to limit cheating and calibrate evaluation for each person. Generative AI also makes it cost-efficient to develop more complex testing formats: story-based situational judgement tests (perhaps even with AI-generated images and videos), problem-based scenarios, and open-world simulations that replicate real-world challenges. Plus, after the exam, AI can help grade the results and generate custom feedback.

In addition to supercharging these conventional testing approaches, advancements in AI open new opportunities for integrated, continuous, and multifactor measures. Combined with sensor technologies (like cameras, proximity detectors, and wearable devices) and **learning analytics** methods, we can now **instrument** assessment environments to collect a constellation of data noninvasively and in situ.

For example, a business negotiation assessment might involve an AI-generated scenario in a virtual world where a learner bargains with corporate stakeholders, each of whom is an AI-driven avatar. In addition to gauging performance at certain gates, the system could collect **behavioural data,** including eye movements, facial expressions, and tone of voice (if spoken dialogue is included). It could also collect behind-the-scenes **clickstream data** about a person's behaviour in a computerised interface, such as where they clicked (did they refer to their notes or swap to an unauthorised window?) and how much time they spent looking at various screens. This level of tracking data is already available today, though early algorithms using it to assess performance have tended to be a bit too crude to depend on and occasionally bias unfairly against certain groups.

Assessment contexts needn't always resemble real-world situations. Using an approach dubbed '**stealth assessment**', Machine Learning algorithms can infer someone's capabilities, such as their problem-solving ability, by watching them play games, like *Plants vs. Zombies 2,* or observing their performance in other innocuous tasks.[35] The data can be collected over time – gradually assembling evidence, possibly from multiple sources, then using AI to make inferences about someone's competence from those observations. (Despite its larcenous name, 'stealth assessment' isn't meant to be covert; rather, its name refers to assessments' operation in the background – which, ethically, the person being assessed should be aware of.)

Stealth assessment and multifactor inferential measures are showing promise in field trials.[36] Neurophysiology data, including facial expressions and vocalisations, are already used in some (controversial) job screen apps.[37] And clickstream data helps proctors confirm test-takers' identities and guard against cheating.[38]

When we add Generative AI into the mix, opportunity expands considerably. Not only can we collect authentic, reliable data and perform inferential and predictive analyses with AI; we'll soon be able to generate on-demand precision testing: fabricating bespoke assessment environments to precisely target the applicable knowledge, skills, or behaviours of each person or team.

[**5**]

The traditional jobs of faculty and staff will shift as Generative AI begins to substitute for low-level test-makers, as it collapses instructional design workflows from months to days, and as it gradually replaces administrative teaching tasks. As with any innovation, we'll both gain and lose. Pieces of our established systems – aspects of authority, control, and veneration – will change. Individual roles across the community will evolve: some jobs will disappear, and new ones will emerge.

We'll see the rise of '**Learning Engineers**' – individuals who use iterative, data-driven processes to combine learning science, technology, analytics, and other human-centred principles to optimise learning outcomes. We'll see an increased need for expert teachers, whose quality can be scaled across thousands of students or modelled and replicated through

AI avatars. (For a budding example of this, have a look at Khanmigo by Khan Academy.) And we'll see more specialists in various forms of EdTech, learning analytics, and psychometrics (the science of human measurement), as we develop more authentic and composite ways to evaluate capability.

We can also hope that a new cadre of ethicists, who understand both humans and algorithms, will emerge to help us advance with care and wisdom. AI holds risk as well as immense promise, and its increasing proliferation puts that double-edged sword into the hands of both sages and charlatans, fools and geniuses, from our traditional academic institutions to the disruptive tech start-ups, and from government programmes to our places of employment. We'll need strong voices to help guide those many actors to embrace their better natures.

[6]

Motivated to seek a commercial edge, many organisations and ambitious professionals are already embracing AI to advance their learning, development, and workforce outcomes. Generative AI will hasten these changes. For example, it's likely to accelerate the consolidation of education, training, and performance. The emergent effect may be a new paradigm of learning, something more fluid and dynamic, less certain and delineated, so that we're learning on the job and performing (simulated) jobs in the (virtual) classroom.

PERSONALISED KNOWLEDGE: A RADICAL COMMODITY?

In his book *Free: The Future of a Radical Price*, Chris Anderson discussed the changing dynamics of information in a digital era.[42]

Published in 2009, the book used a pre–Generative AI Age lens to explore how the traditional model of valuing information has shifted, thanks to the internet-enabled Information Age. Anderson's premise was that given the abundance of information – albeit generic information – available to us, the relative value of general information has dropped to essentially zero.

This devaluation of generic information is particularly evident for digital goods like online discussions, e-news, and software, where copying and distributing is effortless.

Anderson argued that these sorts of '**information as products**' have become easily accessible and replicable, to the point of eliminating their scarcity and, thus, eroding their economic value. He maintained, however, that information personalised for an individual or organisation's unique references, needs, and contexts — that is, '**information as a service**' — was still of immense value and not something easily found or replicated.

Fast-forward to today, where Generative AI is encroaching on that once-safe harbour. As Generative AI matures, the 'information as a service' business model may lose much of the value it once had.

This new paradigm should concern businesses that earn money through the strategic application of technical knowledge, such as management consultants, copy writers, and even attorneys. They've built their livelihoods on transferring general subject-matter expertise (international finance law, for instance) into personal situations (like one particular business contract). The power of Generative AI threatens the scarcity and value of these endeavours.

Unsurprisingly, many traditional educators feel a similar pressure.

We can expect to see more uses of **augmented intelligence**, the integration of AI with human intelligence to enhance our cognitive work. In combination, people and programs can accomplish amazing feats, better than either alone. Even average individuals paired with AI teammates have shown that they can best (human) grandmasters or standalone algorithms.[39]

This gives rise to the notion of **expert generalists**, individuals who possess a broad (but potentially shallow) range of knowledge and skills. Whilst they may have some areas of deep expertise, they're most characteristically experts at boundary spanning, excelling at transdisciplinary skills, critical thinking, creative problem-solving, digital and data literacy, and interdisciplinary collaboration. They're known for their versatility, adaptability, and ability to connect dots across domains.

In other words, we're witnessing a lessening emphasis on 'pure' domain knowledge in favour of more generalisable capability – an era of augmented polymaths. This may be driven, in part, because 'narrow experts' (those individuals at the peak of a specialised but more bounded discipline) are often less adaptable than expert generalists, a potentially fatal flaw in a world of quickening change. Called the 'paradox of expertise', experts' unconscious competence can blind them to changing conditions, even as they grow overconfident. They may also lose their creative spark, falling into patterns of 'functional fixedness' and rigid automaticity.

Philip E. Tetlock, a prominent scientist who studied this paradox, popularised the phrase, 'The fox knows many things; the hedgehog one great thing'. Borrowed from an ancient Greek proverb, that line illustrates two contrasting approaches to expertise.[40] The hedgehog is focused but potentially rigid, whilst the fox is adaptable and holds eclectic expertise. Conventional experts can sometimes be foxes, but expert generalists – especially when augmented by AI – are almost certainly vulpine.

Expert generalists bolstered by AI are increasingly attractive as volatility and complexity grow, and organisations need more agility. The generalists bring adaptability and contextual understanding, whilst the algorithms provide detailed – but narrow – domain expertise relevant to a given situation. 'Augmented generalists' may be the pinnacle of future organisations.

And individual experts aren't the only ones who can be augmented. AI compatriots can join human teams, helping them perform more accurately and efficiently, and AI can help optimise outcomes across teams of people, using their collective performance – which can be input instantly through a brain-computer interface – to identify errant mistakes or compensate for distracted or fatigued team members.[41] This might sound like science fiction, but these Engines of Augmentation are already here, and advancements in Generative AI will merely speed their proliferation.

ENGINES OF DISHONESTY?

The process of learning isn't quick or easy. It's not 'designed' to be tidy. That's not to say that education should be obtuse or training should be demoralising, but without sufficient challenge, learning can't manifest. Muscles need stress to grow stronger, and similarly, our minds need stimulation and provocation to learn.

Naturally, the potential of Generative AI to shortcut learning processes is disconcerting. Learners are ever-motivated to find the pathways of least resistance, like outsourcing essay writing, test taking, and the summarisation of assigned reading to algorithms.

Is that cheating?

The line between cheating and learning is a fine one or, at least, a contextual one. Learners using AI tools to create scaffoldings, explore connections, or navigate ideas may be employing spectacular learning tactics. By conversing with an AI assistant, learners can expand their comprehension, develop their inquiry skills, and mature their meta-cognition (a higher-order thinking skill related to advanced awareness of one's own gaps, capabilities, and needs).

Learners can also overuse AI, relying on it as a crutch whilst their own critical-thinking skills atrophy and their long-term understanding is stunted. AI can summarise a text, but that's not a substitute for reading the book. Equally concerning, generative algorithms aren't 'Engines of Answers'. They're not all-wise, all-seeing, and all-knowing. And although Generative AI can 'make sense', it's not 'my' sense or 'your' sense. Algorithms can't construct the meaning that sits within our heads, even though they can sometimes help us uncover the epiphanies to do so ourselves.

There's also a risk that as learners increasingly depend on Generative AI, their work may become more impersonal. Stories may no longer include individual authenticity, artworks may no longer have a personal touch, and even music compositions can be coldly fabricated by commonplace algorithms. By overusing AI crutches in creative domains, learners may lose opportunities to grow their own voices and imaginations.

All that said, banning the use of AI in learning makes as much sense as banning calculators in algebra or the internet from history class. Those disciplines routinely rely on such digital tools, and AI is – or soon will be – the same.

In retort, someone might ask, 'How can we test students' knowledge or verify trainees' participation if they can easily use Generative AI to complete their homework or fake their attendance at a webinar?' But that's the wrong question. A better question is one that examines our current structures and constraints: 'Are we controlling for the right things?'

If we've devised such fragile structures of learning that it's necessary to encumber learners' capability in order for them to engage, then maybe the fault lies more with the system than with learners' actions. So, perhaps our time would be better spent looking for ways to evolve that system – ways for Generative AI to scaffold learning experiences and take learners to new heights – rather than escalating a classroom arms-race by trying to bar AI's use in learning contexts.

After all, through another lens, 'cheating' might be called 'innovation', and our job as educators and trainers is to prepare learners for the future – a future that will certainly involve Generative AI.

AUGMENTED TRIBES AND (ANTI) SOCIAL LEARNING

Learning comes in many shapes and sizes. Some experiences are fully formal, taking place within the confines of well-structured classes or rigid training programmes; others are grown from our tribal knowledge and practical experiences. **Social learning** makes use of this sort of tacit knowledge. It's imperfect and untidy – at least by the structured and validated notions that formal organisations typically employ – but it tends to be very pragmatic and often extremely valuable.

One of the main mechanisms for sharing tribal knowledge is

dialogue: storytelling, problem-solving, and challenging one another through curiosity and questions. Organisations can help foster these interactions through scaffolded support, where we create collaborative spaces of dialogue as well as more formal gateways to guide sense-making communities and help them find ways to share their insights.

Generative AI can make **Scaffolded Social Learning** more accessible – and in powerful ways.

Consider narrative. Social tribes form and communicate through story. Generative AI tools (like Copilot in Teams or the Zoom AI Companion) can synthesise the co-created narratives of a group, or they can provide a dialogic framework for members to spar with or build upon.

Between tribes or parallel cohorts, Generative AI tools can help compare and contrast narratives to identify divergences. These departures mark points of interest along the landscape of tribal knowledge, because local understanding necessarily deviates from the 'authoritative narrative', so being able to find and compare those differences is often revelatory.

Of course, the stories that create coherence within a group can also erect walls that separate in-group from out-group, which can be problematic if new members want to join an established tribe. Here again, Generative AI can create the necessary scaffolding, empowering us to navigate the stories told by others through prompting and signposting, nudging curious exploration, and surfacing emergent themes from across the community as 'tribal guidebooks' or narrative journeys.

Generative algorithms can be interconnectors, moderators, wayfinders, and alternatively gatekeepers or bridges, helping individuals tap and traverse webs of tribal knowledge.

Potentially, AI might become whole communities.

Historically, dialogue and co-creation have been the domain of individuals operating in social structures. Formal organisations and less formal tribes have respectively held both codified and socially co-created dynamic forms of knowledge. And communities have classically relied on reputation to surface signals amongst the noise, with each tribe requiring idiosyncratic dues in terms of reputation, time, effort, decorum, and culture. Now, it's possible to imagine Generative AI playing every role within a community – essentially for 'free' – at least from a mechanical perspective, creating our own epic narrative, personalised and filled with countless non-player characters with whom we can interact, enabling us to dialogue with ourselves: a kind of *anti*-social learning.

Collaborative in design, but not with others.

A community of one.

Collective in appearance, but alone in practice.

The impacts of this may be interesting. The proliferation of bots across our social learning spaces might strip away essential aspects of challenge or facilitation, as well as scale. They may lull us into patterns of anti-social behaviour or low-effort collaboration, or they might serve as models of better interaction, potentially exemplifying the mechanics of curiosity, engagement, and collaboration. Perhaps they'll diversify our perspectives as we explore unfettered avenues, free of consequence and reputational risks. Or maybe the invasion of the Dialogue Engines into our social communities will fracture trust and undermine the very value they seek to bolster.

The Engines are already in motion, so we'll soon discover whether they're Engines of Collective Growth – strengthening communities and revealing distributed expertise – or Engines of Fragmentation that threaten the fragile authenticity of our social fabric.

HUMBLE ICONOCLASTS

Some learning and development professionals may resent this new reality, but the truth is that the old models were already crumbling from the aftershocks of the Information Age. By now, the rust has set in, and yesterday's deteriorating paradigms won't withstand the quakes of Generative AI.

Yet, many of us hesitate.

Our own experiences, moulded by the paradigms of the past, have indoctrinated us in outmoded forms of education and learning. Our frames of reference were born from those structures. Undoubtedly, the old traditions, dogma, and well-trodden methods have their merits. They've built the intellectual platform on which we stand today, and they foster clarity and consistency across our institutions. But that comfortable familiarity can also blind us to progress. Taken to the extreme, we can become hoarders of outdated truths, suffocating under a bygone age.

Present-day education systems still bear a striking resemblance to those old Prussian schools: production lines that overly emphasise information transfer and are held hostage by assessments that drive monoculture and constraint. Workplace training isn't much better, favouring tidy structures over complex realities and often focussing on incremental skill development rather than preparing workforces for the authentic challenges they'll face.

Whilst we mustn't throw out the wisdom of the past, it's time to humbly acknowledge that the old models, which served us well in their time, are tarnishing. What was once a patina of age and enlightenment has given way to corrosion. It's time to recalibrate our outlook on learning:

- ▸ Do we still require the conventional model of 'school', where time, location, and paper-based teaching reign supreme? What parallel and alternative layers of learning can help us better adapt to the dynamic challenges of our era? If you had a blank slate and a magic wand, what knowledge and skills would you prioritise for future generations, especially knowing that they'll be augmented by AI companions?

- What role do the formal centres of knowledge and authority (such as universities, employers, licensing agencies, and government programmes) play in the future of learning? Should they staunchly defend their legacy against the rising tide of disruptors or seek a harmonious coexistence?

- If we choose to hesitate, waiting and watching how the landscape unfolds, then who will steer the change? And will we appreciate their decisions about the winners and losers, those who profit and those who are exploited, and the human qualities that are elevated versus those we choose to cede to the machines?

Certainly, embracing this ambiguous new reality carries some risks, but if we stand by the wayside, waiting for certainty to emerge before action is taken, then we'll surely be left behind. And, meanwhile, those early adopters – like 'fail-fast' start-ups and avaricious corporations – will have full latitude to make decisions for this sector.

As humans, learning is at our very cores. Our capacity to learn and the learning experiences we've had shape the trajectories of our lives. Our societies are built around institutions of learning, structures of assessment, and incentives for scholastic achievement. Hence, the transformation of learning through AI isn't merely a curiosity for educators or a market disruptor for textbook makers. It stands as a profound upheaval of the human condition, affecting the myriad ways we work, thrive, grow, and discover. Engagement is imperative. This is a conversation in which we all have a stake; it's time to join the dialogue about AI and learning, before the future landscape is decided for us.

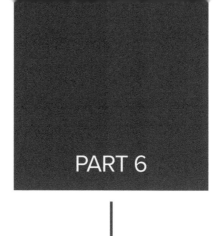

PART 6

A Curious Harvest

With leaps and stumbles, driven by optimism or ideology, curiosity or anxiety, we nonetheless find ourselves here.

Inevitable.

Accelerating down the slippery slope.

One horn sounds. Then another.

Rapidly the air fills with noise: Engines of Creativity, Purpose, or Profit all honking, hooting, chirping, and squawking at one another, whilst all around hands wave. Commentators opine. Alarmists shout. And stewards blow whistles, paradoxically attempting to slow and silence the din whilst adding noise to the cacophony.

We're sliding deeper into a growing dissonance. And with each new signal, we collectively jump in alarm (or glee or greed). It almost doesn't matter whether each new advance is a blaring siren or a purring harmony. We're overloaded, and every addition adds to the jumble, leaving us without space to breathe and reflect, differentiate or categorise. How can we move forward, when every new Engine seems to signal a warning that shocks our systems? The complexity feels overwhelming. And, in all the noise, rational debate quietly dies.

ANXIETY, COMPLEXITY AND DISCOMFORT

It's not uncommon to feel a sense of anxiety in response to Generative AI: fear that it will overtake humans or render our works obsolete, uncertainty over the ever-accelerating societal change, and a growing sense of moral panic.

<u>Moral panic</u> is the feeling that something – typically something inherently 'evil' – is threatening our way of life. An existential threat. It has the connotation of irrationality, although clearly some threats posed by Generative AI aren't fabricated: Bias exists. Unfairness is present. Crimes are being committed.

Already, in a rush to depravity, people are generating images of abuse, whilst others are being robbed of their savings or convinced to believe fabricated news. So, we shouldn't be wide-eyed about it, nor should we be so quick to sound another alarm bell.

We collectively have a poor track record in our applications of moral panic: Dancing Mania of the Mediaeval era, the Red Scare of the 1940s, and the exaggerated fear of Satanism in the 1980s. Famously, and often cited in today's discussions about AI, Socrates even expressed some inklings of panic over the invention of writing. Other inventions, from the telegram to social media, were also predicted to lead to society's downfall. Yet, still we persist.

As captured by Plato, Socrates warned of the moral fracture that writing would bring: 'For this discovery of yours [this gift of letters] will create forgetfulness in the learners' souls, because they will not use their memories, they will trust to the external written characters and not remember of themselves. The specific which you have discovered is an aid not to memory, but to reminiscence, and you give your disciples not truth, but only the semblance of truth; they will be hearers of many things and will have learned nothing; they will appear to be omniscient and will generally know nothing; they will be tiresome company, having the show of wisdom without the reality'.[43]

Nebulous fear spreads like ink in the water. Until we have the benefit of many decades of hindsight, it's difficult to say which concerns are warranted. But we can anticipate that nonspecific angst and knee-jerk reactions are unlikely to serve us well. Change is inevitable, but how we navigate it – how we seek balance between churning adaptation versus rigid adherence to the past – rests with each of us. Should we relax our standards to maximise experimentation and the possibility of the good? Do we accept certain harms simply in the name of progress? Whom do we protect, and what limits do we accept for that security?

There's always a tension at play. Our organisations are constrained and slow to change by design, and often rightly so. We don't want to unravel our systems with each new fad. But there's also a price for being too slow, and when it comes to paradigmatic change, that price may be extinction.

So, what to do? The first step on the path of sustainable progress lies with a willingness to understand ourselves, to engage in solo and social meta-cognition so that we see our motives clearly. Are we pausing wisely to make sense of the landscape? Are we rushing ahead, wearing blindfolds of optimism or glasses tinted by the 'fear of missing out'? Or are we in denial, paralysed by the inevitable weight of complexity and feelings of unease that come from the fracturing of our concepts of familiarity?

It's worth remembering that these perceptions can manifest from emotional, as opposed to strictly structural, origins. Or to put it another way: We mustn't let paper tigers stop our progress because we imagine that they have teeth and claws.

Doing nothing seems like a poor option, and trying to exert control seems infeasible. But if we can overcome this tension and break through the inertia of hesitation, then the next step is to seek knowledge – not necessarily expertise. Because whilst excitement or apprehension may get in the way of our decision-making, the most likely impediment we'll face is simple ignorance.

No one, not even the loudest of voices, has the gift of foresight. No one is a comprehensive expert on AI and its many technical pieces, organisational processes, and rippling effects. Exercise some reasonable doubt of anyone who claims omniscience in this burgeoning space.

Instead, forge forward boldly with curiosity. Curate trusted networks, and have the confidence to share your perceptions and questions, explorations and failures. Each of us has more agency than we may believe, and we can each uncover threads that may grow into pillars within this new reality. But we're unlikely to find that knowledge if we stand apart, waiting and watching from the sidelines.

Sometimes, it's simply important to be in motion: in our work, our thinking, and our imagination. Better to begin building our personal and organisational repertoires of AI fluency – no matter how clumsy or hesitant we might feel – sooner rather than later. Even taking small steps to build a vocabulary and gain some small personal experiences can help. And if we feel a bit unprepared to begin, it's useful to remember that today is as limited as AI will ever be. Its influence expands daily, so it's best to step onto the merry-go-round now, before it spins ever faster.

Individuals and, in particular, organisations may be tempted to outsource their thinking around AI, waiting for technology companies to blaze the trail ahead, to tell us what to think or fear about these new Engines of Capability. Of course, there's nothing wrong with depending upon knowledgeable guides, but as with most things, the trick is finding balance. Avoid ceding too much to others, especially when their profit is on the line.

As Generative AI matures, it will be (and in fact has already been) woven into many of our most familiar applications. It's tempting to simply wait and watch, comfortably spoon-fed Generative AI with software patches and routine updates. But take care to avoid a false sense of security. It's worthwhile to seek out sandboxes for play and experimentation. Some truths are emergent. And we're likely to need both: safety in numbers and scale as well as lived experiences and grassroots innovation. So, each time you make a safe decision, consider also balancing it with a slightly riskier one that helps expose you to the edges and outliers of this new world of possibilities.

Another useful thing to consider when making decisions about Generative AI, particularly in organisational situations, is whether we're seeking optimisation or innovation. Are we happy with a 'Type-1 Change' that accelerates the flow within our existing system, or are we seeking a 'Type-2

Change' that reroutes the pipes entirely?

For instance, do we need a more efficient way to summarise resumes, or would we be better served with a wholly different approach to recruitment? Would we benefit most from AI summarisation of our web-based meetings, or should we consider new ways to meet and tell stories about our collective efforts?

It's worth remembering that our future organisations will not simply be AI-empowered lookalikes of what we have today – the same but slightly faster or better. Instead, it's much more likely that our future structures will have evolved mechanisms of effect, governance, and undertaking. And to uncover that path requires prototyping, experimentation, and the development of a culture of exploration.

The initial waves of Generative AI were mostly led by giant corporations, allowing us (as individual actors) limited agency in what happened. But as the underlying technology becomes commercialised, we find smaller and more diverse innovators are embedding it in creative and niche solutions, many of which are speculative or fragile, and a good number of which will fail or at least prove no better than the status quo. Regardless of the individual outcomes, such innovation-minded temperaments will likely serve us well as we collectively fumble towards the future – so long as we're willing to open ourselves to a bit of curiosity and can keep the imagined claws of panic from our paths.

UNTAMED FUTURES

Will governments keep us safe?

In a word: unlikely.

At least, not through actions solely directed at AI.

Legal and regulatory frameworks are often better at retrospective analysis than at predictive action. And in a global context, we'll likely find that any attempts at regulating AI – whether prescriptive or retroactive – form a patchwork fence that stubborn innovations slip through.

Even amongst those nations and international institutions that are willing to regulate, it's still difficult to do. There are a few obvious 'red lines'. For example, the European Union has banned the use of Generative AI for subliminal or purposeful manipulation. (The EU's AI Act also categorically bans various Machine Learning applications, such as remote biometric identification and social credit systems that classify people based on their social behaviours, socioeconomics, or other personal characteristics.[44])

As we walk back a step from such glaring red lines, however, the boundaries of 'reasonable' safety grow hazier. At a surface level, it might seem that level-headed people would easily agree on certain ideas. For instance, we should have clarity about whether we're dealing with a human or a machine in particular situations. However, precisely *which* situations that tenet applies to is a bit murkier.

Should AI medics identify themselves as such?

Perhaps legal researchers too?

How about online help-desk operators or in-app baristas?

Where do we draw the line, and will our contemporary feelings about the uncanny valley between 'real' and 'artificial' workers seem old-fashioned in years to come? Will future generations find it endearingly quaint that we focused on such distinctions, perhaps in a way similar to how we view the Luddites who baulked at automated factories in the early nineteenth century? [45]

Most people today – but likely not all – would concur with placing some constraints on the kinds of imagery that AI is allowed to produce (a constraint that the most popular visual generators have already implemented).

But, again, where do we collectively draw a hard line?

Is tasteful artistic nudity allowed?

Political satire of authoritarian leaders or religious imagery?

How about the use of celebrities' faces or even our own likenesses, especially when used by others? And what if those 'others' are profiting from those AI-generated materials? The situation lies between complexity and discomfort, with a veil of denial cast over it.

At an abstract technical level, Generative AI isn't too difficult to understand. What it does is comparatively simple in conception: It remixes established ideas to produce new creations. This seemingly uncomplicated concept is so powerful, in large part because of its simplicity and wide generalisability. Similar to how simple machines – levers and screws and the like – form the fundamental building blocks of mechanical engineering, Generative AI might be considered a new and quintessential digital tool, something akin to discovering pulleys. What we'll be able to build or disrupt with this new tool is anyone's guess.

And therein lies the complexity.

When a wholly new capability is given to humankind, with our endless ingenuity, the possibilities are limitless. Our depths of creativity – and of creative delinquency – are unmatched. This alloy of persons and programs is both an opportunity and our greatest area of concern.

It's unlikely that governments can protect us from the innovations brought about by AI. At best, governmental regulation is fighting a series of rear-guard actions that are (at least partially) directed against the wrong front. Because whilst algorithms may be corrupted into Engines of Disinformation or Criminality, it's our own human imaginations and incentives driving their uses. And our capacity for both wit and wickedness – especially now that we're augmented by AI – is peerless.

INTERLUDE FOR
A BIRDSONG

I watch the combine harvester with my son. It's remarkably agile, heading up the field towards us as we stand by the hedge. The giant fans inside the machine vent up through a hatch on its roof, surrounding the vehicle in a haze of dust and roar of moving air.

It comes right up to where we stand, turning on a pinhead on the headland of the field, the driver even finding time to wave at us as he pilots onto a new course. And then, as the vehicle retreats down the field, the blast hits us: the exhaust of chopped straw, husks, and dirt filling the air – and our noses and hair.

As the machine harvests the grain, it casts everything else aside – and we cough and run for cover from the chaff it flings behind. Mechanised, efficient, and leaving us dishevelled and breathless in its wake.

The harvest is a moment of judgement, the culmination of an agrarian year. My mother remembers the old harvest suppers, a party in the village after the crops were safely gathered in. But no more. Whilst harvesting used to be manual and backbreaking work, today it's substantially optimised and scaled. The old hedges separating the networks of mediaeval fields are long gone; the ditches are filled in. Some farmers have even ploughed over the neolithic barrows that once disrupted the straight lines of their geometric planting, figuring that a regulatory fine would be worth the increased yield.

The industrialisation of agriculture has led to plentiful food in many affluent societies. We've created widespread bounty by changing the landscape around us. But our prosperity hasn't come without injury. Indeed, only a few decades prior, the hedge my son and I stood beside would have lain silent, with pesticides and overcultivation having decimated its insect life and driven away the birds whose song (and opportunistic squabbling for leftovers) had serenaded the harvest since the advent of agriculture. But, as our yields grew more efficient, our landscapes became more monocultural and our silent skies filled with the dust of depleted soil.

Then there was something of a turnaround; subsidies for preserving the hedgerows began. We paid people to leave the headlands to wildflowers and let weeds grow in their fields, or even to leave entire farmlands to the fickleness of nature, giving them time to lay fallow and regenerate.

We exploited and suffered, then adapted and adjusted, whilst hoping to find an unsteady balance between progress and collapse. Some doubts still linger as to whether we fully succeeded or acted with enough alacrity. Sometimes, like the birdsong, we don't miss something until it's gone.

A FRACTAL VIEW

Across the arc of human history, we've made uneven progress: long periods of certainty, followed by violent punctuations of fracturing change, unpredictable innovation, and social evolution. And throughout it all, our progress has been intertwined with technology, from the advent of wheels and written words to antibiotics and personal computers. We progress. Technology progresses. But the impacts are not linear.

Sometimes we move ahead in leaps and bounds.

Sometimes things break.

Sometimes we stumble down dark paths.

The conceptual breakthrough of Generative AI gives us a wholly novel capability: a new resource to tap. Like the printing press or the combustion engine, these new Engines have widespread promise, with the possibility of impacting us individually (on a very local human scale) as well as globally, across nearly every system and social structure we've invented thus far.

These AI Engines are just revving up. We're still in the early stages of fluid progress, and as a result, our outlooks are still focused on the minutiae and the immediate. They're kaleidoscopic and fragmented. What visions will we see if we step back from the pixels and let the patterns of progress begin to emerge? It's difficult to say from our present perspectives.

We all have limits to our imaginations, which are substantially coloured by our experiences, dominant cultural norms, and collective narratives. Certain things are familiar to us, and even when we strive for open-mindedness, we simply can't imagine them changing.

However insightful we feel we are, it's likely that each of us is in denial about some forthcoming change. Each of us wants to hold onto the belief that we (ourselves and our roles) are exceptional and inimitable.

Anything to validate ourselves.

But hope doesn't make it true. Just because we – or, rather, the things we do with our hands and minds – used to carry value, there's no cosmic law that says those things will continue to be valuable tomorrow.

Certainly, there will be 'value' available for us in this bold future, but it may sit in different parts of the landscape. The conductors, fusion builders, synthesis engineers, interpreters, storytellers, connectors, and subverters of the future will sit within new roles and spaces.

Things that were a matter of expertise and art are moving into the flow of thought. And as they do so, they warp and transmute our ways of thinking, and – especially in the context of our radically connected Social Age – they allow us to see the world through a kaleidoscope of new ideas, contorted perspectives, and creative lenses.

At their best, these Engines of Story and Song, Artwork and Artifice, don't simply tow us along, substituting their outputs for our thinking. Rather, we can leapfrog between neurons and algorithms, jumping between that which is human and that which is machine – an interplay of organic thought and digital artefact.

This is the unencumbered power of curiosity woven into our practice: thought transposed into art; the creation of individualised meaning incidentally. Like the swallow on the wing, twisting and skimming over the grass – beauty held in the totality of movement, the totality of the flight, an intricate dance, entangled yet graceful.

In the Industrial Age, the machines of productivity and effect, of extraction and transformation, were Engines of Fire – destructive to our natural environment, detrimental to our health, and exerting control from the top of an industrial pyramid, where wealth and power flowed to the summit.

But these new Engines are different, or they have the opportunity to be – often operating silently, diversified (as opposed to standardised), complementary to human operators (as opposed to hazardously antagonistic). Synergistic. Things that were hard become easy; complexity is abstracted away or hidden. New things emerge.

And that's our task: to find the new spaces, the new purpose.

It seems unlikely that we can forge ahead without disruption, but we'll weather those waves of change brought about by Generative AI and its fellow Engines of Engagement. We can live with it or – dare we imagine? – thrive through the disruption they herald.

Perhaps we can find a way to reap the
harvest and still hear the birdsong.

Illustrating *Engines of Engagement*

For a book about Generative AI, a book that explores the impacts our new Engines of Engagement have on creativity and artistic value, we wanted to do something special with the illustrations.

Julian illustrates all of his work, and for him, the process of illustration is inherent to the act of thinking. He often creates the illustrations before fully articulating his ideas – in that way, the act of creation becomes almost a collaboration between the linguistic and artistically intuitive parts of his brain. A dialogue between science and art, words and images.

But the dialogue (trilogue!) of this book is different, and hence, so is its artwork.

Not only have we three authors worked together to build the illustrations; we also used a process that incorporates Generative AI. Typically, that process looked something like this: In our weekly 'writing cafe' sessions, we'd identify key concepts to illustrate. Later, Sae and Geoff would work with one of the Engines of Art to generate prototype designs around those topics. We used a mix of Adobe Firefly and Midjourney. Compared to manual illustration, this process was prolific, but it still took some time to reach the outcomes we wanted. As Geoff explained:

I used a mix of Midjourney and Firefly, playing with both to try to capture the visual idea I had in my head. I'd start with one tool, then use the images it produced as seeds in the other. My process involved two parallel tasks: First, finding a style that I liked. I had to find phrases to define the style we were creating, such as 'whimsical' and 'hand-drawn'. Second, visualising what I had in mind. Here, I picked themes from our written work that popped out at me, then manually sketched or imagined how I'd like to visualise those ideas. Once I had that, I entered into a dialogue with the Engine, trying to explain in words the essence of my vision. It took quite a few iterations until I reached an agreement with the Engine on how we both imagined it to look!

I felt empowered, inspired, and sometimes surprised.

Making the draft illustrations required trial-and-error and creative vision – albeit enabled by a grandmaster, super-art brain. Generative AI allowed us to prototype at lightning speed and experiment with different styles. Working with these tools was exhilarating and empowering, a remarkable union between human and machine. And it was a *union.* Although the barriers to using these Engines of Creativity are low, we nonetheless needed to put effort towards producing meaningful materials, especially if we wanted them to align with our expectations.

Over time, we began to use our own completed images (things we'd previously drawn and edited) as 'references'. In other words, we could upload our own artwork into, say, Firefly, and it would generate outputs with similar visual elements. This allowed us to build a portfolio around a particular 'voice'.

The end result of this 'generation' phase was a lot of unusable images, along with a few dozen contenders that we reviewed together. Julian picked from these, selecting individual images to use as inspiration for his hand-drawn artwork, which he created using a digital stylus and the Paper app on his iPad. This part, at least, followed his typical approach to illustrating.

Once Julian sketched a new design, with some trepidation, he'd pass those images back to Sae and Geoff for review. Sometimes we'd iterate a bit, and we even abandoned a few concepts at this point. But once we were satisfied with a sketch (or, at least, convinced to give a particular design a try), the next stages of digital creation began.

Sae is an experienced graphic designer, and she built on

Generative AI

Digital Painting in Paper

Digitally Enhanced

Julian's artwork using Adobe Photoshop and Illustrator. She added original elements, such as detailing and texture, as well as some digital magic using Photoshop filters or the built-in Generative Fill function to extend or tweak parts of Julian's sketches.

Here's an example of this evolution: Our 'Blue Lady' illustration, which you can find in Part 4 of this book, started in Firefly. Sae generated the initial design using phrases from the 'Worshipping the Word' subsection, such as 'language forms the conduit between our inner and outer worlds' and 'our reality is built of language'. Sae iterated and tweaked the settings until the Blue Lady prototype was created.

Next, Julian recreated the concept as a much cleaner (digital) watercolour painting via the Paper app. Gone are the finer details and sea of words, but in their place a clearer focus on the flowing blue lines has emerged. As an aside, until this adventure, Julian had always declared he couldn't paint faces. Now it seems, prompted by AI, he's found a new talent!

In the third image, Sae has taken Julian's Paper painting back into Photoshop, where she used Generative Fill to expand the image into a portrait layout, generating the Blue Lady's neck. This is an excellent demonstration of how AI has quickly become a commoditised tool in the digital artist's toolbox.

Sae also used Generative AI to tweak the Blue Lady's lips, making them a bit closer to anatomically correct. She also added the 'shards' around the image, some digital ink splatters, texture, and drop shadows. Together, these details came to define much of our style.

For another example, consider the combine harvester image found in Part 6 of this book. It followed a similar path. Plus, for the combine harvester, we borrowed elements directly from other artworks to inform the final version.

Notice those radial lines in the final image? They were skilfully repurposed from an early sketch that Julian created for a different part of the book. Thanks to Sae's digital-image mastery, we were able to surgically replace the dark sky in combine harvester painting with a more vibrant and energetic pattern.

Generative AI

Digital Painting in Paper

As we progressed through our images, discovering our synergy and collective visual grammar, our style evolved. After a handful of images, we settled on a palette and some characteristic design details, which Sae amusingly labelled as our 'fractured' aesthetic.

Ultimately, the twenty images in this book are something that none of us could have created alone, not even with the assistance of these amazing Engines of Art. Ironically, that statement touches on a vein of 'human exceptionalism' that we critically explored in Part 3, but unequivocally no computer could have created these – given the following caveats.

Our creative process was rather slow and inefficient. The book would have been quicker, probably more consistent,

Image with the Radial Lines   Digitally Enhanced

and arguably even 'better' if we'd taken us humans out of the equation. But those human elements – the imperfections we create and the experiences that we, the artists, have gained from the process – are, at least partially, the point of the art. Value came from the collaboration, both with AI and amongst ourselves. In a very real sense the evolution of the art, the synthesis of styles, and the artefacts that we created influenced our writing and thinking, and those ripples affected the landscape that we (as authors) and you (as readers) have travelled.

In this way, art is the journey, not simply the destination, and we're grateful that you took that journey by our sides and, maybe, were even a bit inspired by our AI-enabled, human-made – and often quite quirky – original illustrations. ★

Additional Contributors

These authors kindly shared their thoughts about
Generative AI in short essays throughout this book.

Donald Clark is an entrepreneur, investor, author, speaker, and blogger with 40 years of experience in learning technologies. He's helped start and direct three AI and learning companies, and has contributed to several others, and he literally wrote the book on AI in learning with *AI for Learning* published in 2021.

Donald's other books include *Learning Experience Design* (2022), *Learning Technologies* (2023), *Learning in the Metaverse* (2023) and *Artificial Intelligence for Learning: Using Generative AI,* scheduled for release in 2024. His blog is located at https://donaldclarkplanb.blogspot.com.

Mark Oehlert is relentlessly curious. As a trained anthropologist and historian, Mark has translated his background into delivering innovative, transformative results. He has a track record in designing, developing, and launching learning and innovation programs at enterprise scale that increase engagement and retention and drive organizational performance. For example, Mark has run learning and innovation programs at the US Department of Defense and Amazon, and he led the social impact program at Unity 3D.

Mark thrives in creative, collaborative environments and embraces the ambiguity that often comes with that. Currently, Mark is an Innovation Fellow at the Institute for Innovation in Large Organizations. Follow Mark at https://markoehlert. substack.com.

Marc Zao-Sanders is the founder and CEO of filtered.com, a tech company that develops AI to understand learning content in order to upskill people. He's passionate about algorithms, learning, content, AI, thinking differently, how brains operate in general, and, in particular, how his own brain works.

Marc holds a degree in Maths & Philosophy from Oxford and has founded two social enterprises that helped non-privileged young people with their education and career aspirations, choices, and success.

He's a regular contributor to *Harvard Business Review* and other publications, usually talking about AI, learning, or *timeboxing*. He's just written *Timeboxing: The Power of Doing One Thing at a Time,* published by Penguin Random House in January 2024.

Marc lives in North London with his wife, three kids, two cats, and two dogs.

Endnotes

1   Hoffmann, J., Borgeaud, S., Mensch, A., Buchatskaya, E., Cai, T., Rutherford, E., et al. (2022). Training compute-optimal large language models, *arXiv: 2203, 15556v1*. https://doi.org/10.48550/arXiv.2203.15556

2   Schreiner, M. (2023, June 11). GPT-4 architecture, data sets, costs and more leaked. *The Decoder*. https://the-decoder.com/gpt-4-architecture-datasets-costs-and-more-leaked

3   Ibid, Schreiner, 2023.

4   Shivakumar, S. & Wessner, C. (2022, June 8). *Semiconductors and national defense: What are the stakes?* Center for Strategic and International Studies. https://www.csis.org/analysis/semiconductors-and-national-defense-what-are-stakes

5   Huang, K. & O'Regan, S.V. (2023, Sept. 5). Inside Meta's AI drama: Internal feuds over compute power. *The Information*. https://www.theinformation.com/articles/inside-metas-ai-drama-internal-feuds-over-compute-power

6   Clearly, we've contrived this comparative example. In practice, we're relatively certain that Mercedes-Benz offers generous legroom, and we trust that no panel vans were harmed in the making of this analogy.

7   Dastin, J. (2018, Oct. 10). Amazon scraps secret AI recruiting tool that showed bias against women. *Reuters*. https://www.reuters.com/article/us-amazon-com-jobs-automation-insight-idUSKCN1MK08G

8   Heaven, W.D. (2020, July 17). Predictive policing algo-
     rithms are racist: They need to be dismantled. *MIT
     Technology Review.* https://www.technologyreview.
     com/2020/07/17/1005396/predictive-policing-algo-
     rithms-racist-dismantled-machine-learning-bias-crimi-
     nal-justice

9   Alba, D. (2022, Dec. 8). OpenAI chatbot spits out biased
     musings, despite guardrails. *Bloomberg.* https://www.
     bloomberg.com/news/newsletters/2022-12-08/chatgpt-
     open-ai-s-chatbot-is-spitting-out-biased-sexist-results

10   Nicoletti, L. & Bass, D. (2023, June 14). Humans are bi-
     ased; Generative AI is even worse. *Bloomberg.* https://
     www.bloomberg.com/graphics/2023-generative-ai-bias

11   Each of these tokens is converted (by a single-layer neural
     net) into an embedding vector (of length 768 for GPT-2
     and 12,288 for ChatGPT's GPT-3). See: Wolfram, S. (2023,
     Feb. 14). What is ChatGPT doing...and why does it work?
     Stephen Wolfram Writings [blog]. https://writings.stephen-
     wolfram.com/2023/02/what-is-chatgpt-doing-and-why-
     does-it-work

12   Vincent, J. (2016, March 24). Twitter taught Microsoft's AI
     chatbot to be a racist asshole in less than a day. *The Verge.*
     https://www.theverge.com/2016/3/24/11297050/tay-micro-
     soft-chatbot-racist

13   OpenAI. (2023, March 27). GPT-4 Technical Report. *arXiv:
     2303, 08774.* https://doi.org/10.48550/arXiv.2303.08774

14   Borak, M. (2023, June 14). EU Parliament approves AI Act
     amid heated biometrics debates. *Biometric Update.* https://
     www.biometricupdate.com/202306/eu-parliament-ap-
     proves-ai-act-amid-heated-biometrics-debates

15 Soare, S.R. (2021, Nov. 19). Algorithmic power, NATO and artificial intelligence. *International Institute for Strategic Studies.* https://www.iiss.org/sv/online-analysis/military-balance/2021/11/algorithmic-power-nato-and-artificial-intelligence

16 Regarding China: Davidson, H. (2023, Feb. 23). 'Political propaganda': China clamps down on access to ChatGPT. *The Guardian.* https://www.theguardian.com/technology/2023/feb/23/china-chatgpt-clamp-down-propaganda

Regarding other nations: Martindale, J. (2023, April 12). These are the countries where ChatGPT is currently banned. *Digital Trends.* https://www.digitaltrends.com/computing/these-countries-chatgpt-banned

17 OpenAI. (2023, July 25). GPT-4 vs GPT-3.5 exam scores: AI performance against humans. *ChatGPT Blog* [blog]. https://chatgptplus.blog/gpt4-test-scores

18 Hersche, M., Zeqiri, M., Benini, L. et al. A neuro-vector-symbolic architecture for solving Raven's progressive matrices. *Nature Machine Intelligence 5,* 363–375 (2023). https://doi.org/10.1038/s42256-023-00630-8

19 Metaculus, an online forecasting platform that aggregates human predictions, shows that many respondents predict that Artificial General Intelligence will be invented around end of this decade (that is, by around 2030). They define AGI as 'a single unified software system that can...

[1] reliably pass a 2-hour, adversarial Turing test with text, images, and audio files...

[2] has general robotic capabilities, of the type able to...satisfactorily assemble a (or the equivalent of a) circa-2021 Ferrari 312 T4 1:8 scale automobile model...

[3] high competency at a diverse fields of expertise, as measured by achieving at least 75% accuracy in every task and 90% mean accuracy across all tasks...

[4] able to get top-1 strict accuracy of at least 90.0% on interview-level problems found in the APPS benchmark...

[5] can, for example, explain its reasoning on a Q&A task, or verbally report its progress and identify objects during model assembly.

See: https://www.metaculus.com/questions/5121/ date-of-artificial-general-intelligence

A survey of AI experts from 2022 predicts that there's a 50% chance AGI will be invented in the next 37 years. See: Stein-Perlman, Z., Weinstein-Raun, B., & Grace, K. (2022, Aug. 3). 2022 expert survey on progress in AI. *AI Impacts.* https://aiimpacts.org/2022-expert-survey-on-progress-in-ai

Finally, see this summary of AGI expectation dates: Dilmegani C. (2023, Oct. 2). *When will singularity happen? 1700 expert opinions of AGI [2023].* AI Multiple. https://research.aimultiple.com/artificial-general-intelligence-singularity-timing

20   Searle, J. (1980). Minds, brains, and programs. *Behavioral and Brain Sciences, 3*(3), 417–424. https://doi.org/10.1017/S0140525X00005756

21   For example, see Chalmers, D. J. (1996). *The Conscious Mind: In Search of a Fundamental Theory.* Oxford University Press.

22   Damasio, A.R. (1994). *Descartes' Error: Emotion, Reason, and the Human Brain.* US: GP Putnam.

23 The field of Affective Computing was pioneered, in large part, by Rosalind W. Picard; see, e.g., Picard, R.W. (2000). *Affective Computing.* Boston, MA: MIT Press Direct. https://doi.org/10.7551/mitpress/1140.001.0001

24 Harrison, M. (2023, April 28). We interviewed the engineer Google fired for saying its AI had come to life. *Futurism.* https://futurism.com/blake-lemoine-google-interview

25 Clark, D. (2023). *Learning Technology: A Complete Guide for Learning Professionals.* UK: Kogan Page.

26 As quoted by Andreessen, M. (2023, Oct. 16). *The techno-optimist manifesto.* Andreessen Horowitz [blog]. https://a16z.com/the-techno-optimist-manifesto

27 Stodd, J. (2019, Dec. 19). The socially dynamic organisation ['domain to dynamic' pt 7]. *Julian Stodd's Learning Blog* [blog]. https://julianstodd.wordpress.com/2019/12/19/the-socially-dynamic-organisation-domain-to-dynamic-pt-7

28 Stodd, J. (2022, Jan. 26). The context of the Social Age. *Julian Stodd's Learning Blog* [blog]. https://julianstodd.wordpress.com/2022/01/26/the-context-of-the-social-age

29 Stodd, J. (2022). *The Socially Dynamic Organisation: A New Model of Organisational Design.* UK: Sea Salt Publishing. https://seasaltlearning.com/the-socially-dynamic-organisation-guidebook

30 Stodd, J. (2014). *The Social Leadership Handbook.* UK: Julian Stodd at Smashwords. https://seasaltlearning.com/social-leadership-handbook-second-edition

    See also, Stodd, J. (2022). *The Social Learning Guidebook.* UK: Sea Salt Publishing. https://seasaltlearning.com/the-social-learning-guidebook

31   For example, see Gao, Y. (2023). *The Potential of Adaptive Learning Systems to Enhance Learning Outcomes: A Meta-Analysis.* (Doctoral thesis, U. of Alberta). https://doi.org/10.7939/r3-a6xd-m403

Gao examined 77 empirical studies on adaptive learning systems and found, on average, they produce an effect size of 1.48 (mean). For reference, any effect size over 0.25 is considered useful, and any effect size over 0.8 is considered 'large' and can be easily observed with the naked eye.

32   Fletcher, J.D., & Morrison, J.E. (2014). *Accelerating development of expertise: a digital tutor for navy technical training* [technical report]. Arlington, VA: Institute for Defense Analyses.

As a comparison, effect sizes over 1σ roughly equate to an increase of learner performance from the 50th to the 84th percentile, and effect sizes over 2σ are like an increase from the 50th to the 98th percentile.

33   Richards, J. & Dede, C. (2020, Oct. 26). *The 60-year curriculum: A strategic response to a crisis.* Educause Review. https://er.educause.edu/articles/2020/10/the-60-year-curriculum-a-strategic-response-to-a-crisis

34   Typically, David J. Weiss and Nancy E. Betz are credited with pioneering computer-adaptive testing. See: Weiss, D.J. & Betz, N.E. (1973). *Ability measurement: Conventional or adaptive?* (Research Report 73–1). Minneapolis: University of Minnesota, Department of Psychology. https://files.eric.ed.gov/fulltext/ED077933.pdf

35   Shute, V. & Ventura, M. (2013). *Stealth assessment: Measuring and supporting learning in video games.* Boston, MA: MIT Press.

36 For examples of stealth assessment, refer to ibid. Shute and Ventura, 2013. For an example of multi-modal learning analytics employed in a physical (Army) exercise, e.g., see Vatral, C., Biswas, G., Mohammed, N., & Goldberg, B.S. (2022). Automated assessment of team performance using multimodal Bayesian learning analytics. In *Proceedings of the 2022 Interservice/Industry Training, Simulation and Education Conference.* Arlington, VA: National Training and Simulation Association.

37 For example, see Zetlin, M. (n.d.). AI Is now analyzing candidates' facial expressions during video job interviews. *Inc.* https://www.inc.com/minda-zetlin/ai-is-now-analyzing-candidates-facial-expressions-during-video-job-interviews.html

38 For an example of identity verification from clickstream behaviour, see Vamosi, S., Reutterer, T., & Platzer, M. (2022). A deep recurrent neural network approach to learn sequence similarities for user-identification. *Decision Support Systems, 155,* 113718.

For examples of using clickstream behaviours to support academic integrity, see: Mortati, J., & Carmel, E. (2021). Can we prevent a technological arms race in university student cheating? *Computer, 54*(10), 90-94.

… or see Alexandron, G., Berg, A., & Ruipérez-Valiente, J. A. (2023). A general purpose anomaly-based method for detecting cheaters in online courses. *IEEE Transactions on Learning Technologies,* pp. 1–12. https://doi.org/10.1109/TLT.2023.3297132

39 Kasparov, G. (2017). *Deep thinking: Where machine intelligence ends and human creativity begins.* UK: PublicAffairs.

40 The ancient Greek poet Archilochus originally wrote about foxes and hedgehogs, but Philip E. Tetlock (among others) helped to popularize the idea in modern times. For example, see: Tetlock, P. E. (2017). *Expert Political Judgment: How Good Is It? How Can We Know? New Edition.* UK: Princeton University Press.

41 Poli, R. (2023). Super-human and super-AI cognitive augmentation of human and human-AI teams assisted by brain computer interfaces. In *Proceedings of the Genetic and Evolutionary Computation Conference.* New York: Association for Computing Machinery. https://doi.org/10.1145/3583131.3603554

42 Anderson, C. (2009). *Free: The future of a radical price.* US: Hachette Books.

43 Konnikova, M. (2012, April 30). On writing, memory, and forgetting: Socrates and Hemingway take on Zeigarnik. *Scientific American.* https://blogs.scientificamerican.com/literally-psyched/on-writing-memory-and-forgetting-socrates-and-hemingway-take-on-zeigarnik

44 European Parliament. (2023, May 11). AI Act: a step closer to the first rules on Artificial Intelligence (Ref.: 20230505IPR84904). *Press Room.* https://www.europarl.europa.eu/news/en/press-room/20230505IPR84904/ai-act-a-step-closer-to-the-first-rules-on-artificial-intelligence

45 We've referenced the Luddites, with the intent of evoking the mental image of someone fighting against the progress of technology, but the reference is a bit unfair to history. While the Luddites destroyed machines and rioted over automated factories, their primary drivers were social and economic. For example, see Conniff, R. (2011, March). *What the Luddites really fought against.* Smithsonian Magazine. https://www.smithsonianmag.com/history/what-the-luddites-really-fought-against-264412

Additional Reading

SEA SALT PUBLISHING

Sea Salt Publishing is an independent publisher specialising in works exploring aspects of the Social Age. The 'Social Age' was defined by Julian Stodd in 2014 as the new context of our lives and work – a landscape of radical connectivity, diverse ecosystems of technology, a disruption of legacy  power – where much of the value is found at the intersection of formal and social systems. At Sea Salt Publishing, we publish research-led, creative, and ambitious works relevant to Social Age across a variety of formats, from beautiful hardback books through to practical guides and into disruptive and challenging 'zines'.

OTHER BOOKS BY JULIAN STODD

The Humble Leader is a guided reflection into our personal humility as a social leader.

OTHER BOOKS BY JULIAN STODD (CONT.)

The Social Leadership Handbook, 2nd edition explores the intersection of formal and social authority, and it considers the importance of this in the context of the Social Age.

Social Leadership: My First 100 Days is a practical, guided, reflective journey of 100 days of activity, with each including provocations, questions, and actions. You fill in the book as you go. It's accompanied by a set of 100 podcasts.

Power and Potential is an enquiry framework: a series of sixteen questions that, together, provide a space to explore. The subject of the exploration is power – the power that underpins leadership in both formal and social spaces.

The Guidebook Series – Ever-expanding series of short, research-based, practical, and applied Social Age Guidebooks

The Socially Dynamic Organisation presents a new type of organisation, one that's lightweight and rapidly adaptable, that thrives in times of constant change, and that respects the old but embraces the new.

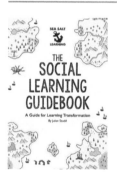

The Social Learning Guidebook provides a practical overview for the principles and design techniques of Social Learning in a modern organisation.

The Trust Guidebook explores our extensive research into the landscape of trust, and it offers seventy-two questions that leaders can use with their teams.

OTHER BOOKS BY JULIAN STODD (CONT.)

The Community Builder Guidebook brings you practical ideas to create engaged and dynamic Social Learning Communities and Communities of Practice.

To the Moon and Back: Leadership Reflections from Apollo shares eight key stories about the Apollo programme, alongside Julian's personal reflections about what this means for leadership in the Social Age.

Quiet Leadership is an exploration of leadership in the smallest of things: our mindset, our words, and our actions in every single day.

OTHER BOOKS BY JULIAN STODD (CONT.)

Finding Your Campfire helps remote teams through the exploration of three themes: packing your backpack, leading the expedition, and being together apart.

CONTINUE THE CONVERSATION

We'd love to hear what you thought about this book! Send us a message, follow our work, and be part of our community.

Engage with Sea Salt Learning at www.seasaltlearning.com or get in touch at hello@seasaltlearning.com. You can also read Julian's daily blog at www.julianstodd.wordpress.com, watch his sixty-second *Social Leadership Daily* videos on Substack at dailyquestions.substack.com, and join weekly deep-dive explorations of *The Captain's Log* at https://social-age.substack.com.

Follow us for updates on LinkedIn, look for Julian Stodd, Sae Schatz, Geoff Stead, and Sea Salt Learning. Or find us on X: @JulianStodd, @SaeSchatz, @geoffstead, and @SeaSaltLearning.

OTHER BOOKS BY SAE SCHATZ

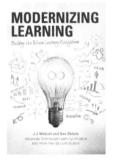

Modernizing Learning: Building the Future Learning Ecosystem, co-authored with JJ Walcutt and dozens of contributors, covers the foundations and futures of technology-enabled lifelong learning. It's freely available at www.adlnet.gov.

Who the F*** Wants to be President: My Year of Living Politically is a humorous true story. Join JJ Walcutt on the campaign trail as she tries to make sense of American politics, government, and civic engagement.

OTHER BOOKS BY GEOFF STEAD

You already have it! You're holding in your hands Geoff's first physical book. Further writing can be located via Scholar and LinkedIn, or search online to find his recent keynotes.

Milton Keynes UK
Ingram Content Group UK Ltd.
UKHW020619191223
434598UK00002B/21

9 781738 448203